DAILY WISDOM · Léann an Lae

DAILY WISDOM

 Léann an Lae

Irish Proverbs and Sayings
for Each Day of the Year

John Quinn

VERITAS

Published 2020 by
Veritas Publications
7–8 Lower Abbey Street
Dublin 1, Ireland
publications@veritas.ie
www.veritas.ie

ISBN 978 1 84730 960 0

10 9 8 7 6 5 4 3 2 1

Eagarthóireacht Ghaeilge: Breandán Ó Raghallaigh KSS KC*HS

Design by Pádraig McCormack
Printed in Ireland by Watermans Printers Ltd, Cork

*Veritas books are printed on paper made from the wood pulp of managed forests.
For every tree felled, at least one tree is planted, thereby renewing natural
resources.*

Ní féidir an seanfhocal a shárú!
You cannot beat the proverb!

CONTENTS

———∞∽———

INTRODUCTION
Réamhrá

Seanfhocail. Old words. Wise sayings that became proverbs. In my primary-school days I remember struggling with the *Vere Foster Handwriting Copybooks* as we copied out headlines in English – 'All that glistens is not gold' – and *ceannlínte* in Irish – *Tosach maith leath na hoibre* (Well begun is half done).

Later, in secondary school, we were advised of the value of including a few *seanfhocail* in the *aiste* (essay). *Ní neart go cur le chéile* (There is strength in unity). *Níl aon tinteán mar do thinteán féin* (There's no place like home).

It was in adulthood, however, that I came to appreciate fully the beauty of *seanfhocail* as repositories of wisdom and lore – *An rud is annamh is iontach* (What's seldom is wonderful) – and as sharp observations of the human condition and the world about us – *Ní hé lá na gaoithe lá na scolb* (The windy day is not the day for thatching) – all expressed with great accuracy and concision. There is also clever wordplay – *Is fearr an tsláinte ná na táinte* (Health is better than wealth) – and music in their sounds – *Filleann an feall ar an bhfeallaire* (Curses come home to roost).

The *seanfhocail* come from an oral tradition of centuries past, a time when Ireland and its people were predominantly agricultural, poor and Catholic. Consequently the proverbs allude to farming life, nature and weather, food and drink, wealth and poverty, health and death, the power of God and the Church, pastimes and pleasures, fortune and misfortune, animals and people. While a number of the *seanfhocail* have passed their sell-by date – *Is dána bean ná muc agus is dána an mhuc ná an diabhal* (A woman is more stubborn than a pig and a pig is more stubborn than the devil) – many of them retain their wisdom and relevance for today's world. *Tá gach duine lách go dtéann bó ina gharraí* (Everyone's kind until a cow breaks into their garden). *Sceitheann fíon an fhírinne* (Wine loosens the tongue). *De réir a chéile a thógtar na caisleáin* (Rome wasn't built in a day).

The *seanfhocail* are so integral to our history and our personality as a people. In recent years I have toyed with the idea of making a collection of these sayings, partly out of a fear that many of them would be lost to succeeding generations. What spurred me into action was listening to the wonderful gaelic games commentator on TG4, Brian Tyers, specifically to his comments on the Galway–Kerry 2019 All-Ireland Minor Football semi-final. There are only minutes to go and Galway lead by a few points, but, as Brian points out, *Ní breac go port é!* It's not a trout until it's (landed) on the bank! It's not over till it's over! What a marvellous expression, used so expertly and perfectly in the heat of battle. I made it even more alliterative by changing it to *Ní breac go bruach é*. It convinced me of the need to put together a collection of such sayings; hence this book.

The book offers a *seanfhocal* for each day of the year. A short explanation or commentary is attached, concluding with a practical exercise, *Bain triail as* (Give it a try), which shows how to extend your Irish vocabulary by picking up on a particular word in the *seanfhocail*. Another exercise included at the end of each month – *Focailín* – will help to build further on your vocabulary.

This is not a textbook, however. It is simply an anthology that pays homage to a people and their language, acknowledging the wisdom and lore that was perfected in a living language over centuries. We have a duty to preserve it, not just in books, but in our daily living. So don't be afraid to make use of a *seanfhocal* whenever an opportunity arises – in your daily (English) conversation, in texts, emails, letters.

BAIN TRIAIL AS

Ní breac go bruach é!

JANUARY

Eanáir

1. TOSACH MAITH
LEATH NA hOIBRE

A good start is half the work. Well begun is half done! A New Year brings resolutions, new beginnings. Making a start is all-important. Even though another *seanfhocal* says, *Bíonn gach tosach lag* (Every beginning is weak), at least it is a start. Make that effort!

⟿ BAIN TRIAIL AS ⟿

Táim réidh chun oibre. I am ready for work.

2. NÍL TUILE DÁ MHÉID NACH dTRÁNN

Even the heaviest flood or tide (*tuile*) recedes. Everything passes – the darkest hour, the heaviest blow, the longest day. We are told that in ancient Greece there was a contest to find a sentence that would always be true. The winning sentence was, 'This too will pass.'

~ BAIN TRIAIL AS ~

Cá mhéad atá ar sin? How much is that?

3. NÍOR BHRIS FOCAL MAITH FIACAIL RIAMH

A good word never broke a tooth. Sometimes, maybe in defeat, the hard or bitter word comes more easily to us. Begrudgery is often seen as an Irish trait. Far better to be gracious and find a 'good word' of praise or congratulations. It won't harm you!

Bhris sé mo chroí. He broke my heart.

4. BÍONN SIÚLACH SCÉALACH

The one who travels has the stories. *Siúlach* literally means one who walks. This *seanfhocal* refers to a distant time when people travelled by foot and so it was the travellers like the poet Raftery and the labourers, the peddlers, the scholars, who carried the *scéalta* (stories), even if they came only from the next parish. Now with global travel, the stories range from Kathmandu to Killorglin.

Siúl liom tamall. Walk awhile with me.

5. IS MAITH AN SCÉALAÍ AN AIMSIR

Time reveals many things. Literally, time is a good storyteller. This is one of many *seanfhocail* that promote the virtue of patience. So stay calm. All in good time. Everything will be revealed. Time will tell.

⌒ BAIN TRIAIL AS ⌒

Aon scéal? Any news?

6. IS ANSA LE DIA GUÍ NÁ GOL

God prefers prayer to crying. Moaning about your misfortune won't get you anywhere. Try a little prayer instead. As my mother loved to say, 'Get down on your knees and give thanks you're still on your feet!'

⌒ BAIN TRIAIL AS ⌒

Guí orainn! Pray for us.

7. NÍ hUASAL NÁ hÍSEAL ACH THUAS SEAL AGUS THÍOS SEAL

Life has its ups and downs (*thuas/thíos*). It's not a question of being lordly (*uasal*) or lowly (*íseal*).

Regardless of rank, life brings high points and low points to all. It's a matter of coping with them.

BAIN TRIAIL AS

Chaith mé seal i Sasana.
I spent a while in England.

8. CHUIR SÉ AN DUBH INA GHEAL ORM

He deceived me. Literally, he convinced me black was white. We have all met this person, the 'smooth operator' who spun a yarn that was entirely believable. *Seachain duine mar sin* (Avoid such a person).

BAIN TRIAIL AS

Dubh is dubh. Out and out.

9. NÍ RAIBH AIR ACH TAOBH DEN BHRÍSTE

He only wore half the trousers. He wasn't the boss. This one comes from the memoir of Peig Sayers. In Peig's time, 'wearing the trousers' would be an exclusively male domain, so wearing 'half the trousers' would be a breakthrough for women. That, of course, was long ago!

⟊ BAIN TRIAIL AS ⟋

Taobh amuigh de sin. Outside of that.

10. TÁ BODHAIRE UÍ LAOIRE AIR

He's as deaf as O'Leary – whoever poor O'Leary was. He is as deaf as a post. Often used as a curse: *Bodhaire Uí Laoire ort* (May you be as deaf as O'Leary)!

⟊ BAIN TRIAIL AS ⟋

Tá mé bodhar leis an gceol sin.
That music has me deaf.

11. IS LEOR NOD DON EOLACH

A hint is enough for the intelligent person. You don't have to spell it out. A good maxim for would-be writers. Don't overwrite! Sometimes it's enough to suggest, to leave something to imagination and intelligence.

⤳ BAIN TRIAIL AS ↩

Is leor sin. That's enough.

12. GO n-ÉIRÍ AN BÓTHAR/AN LÁ LEAT

May your journey/your day be successful. Literally, may the road/day rise with you. A message of goodwill for anyone setting out on a venture or a journey. From *éirigh*, meaning to rise or become.

⤳ BAIN TRIAIL AS ↩

D'éirigh mé go moch ar maidin.
I rose early this morning.

13. IS OLC AN CHEARC
NÁ SCRÍOBANN DI FÉIN

It's a poor hen that doesn't scratch for herself. We should be able to provide for ourselves. Be independent! Find a way to look after yourself, as the hen does by scratching around for food.

⟿ BAIN TRIAIL AS ⟾

Is olc an scéal é. It's a sad state of affairs.

14. TAR ÉIS A THUIGTEAR
GACH BEART

After things happen, they are understood. It's easy to be wise after the event, because hindsight is a wonderful thing.

⟿ BAIN TRIAIL AS ⟾

Ní thuigim focal! I don't understand a word!

15. NÍ FIÚ TRÁINÍN É

He's not worth a straw. He's totally useless. Our ancestors seemed to delight in putting a person down. There are many variations on the above theme. *Ní fiú biorán buí é* (He's not worth a yellow pin). *Ní fiú seile na cuaiche é* (He's not worth a cuckoo spit). A cuckoo spit, as Patrick S. Dinneen, who in 1904 published his famous Irish–English dictionary, *Foclóir Gaedhilge agus Béarla*, delights in telling us, is 'a congeries of minute parasites on plants'.

BAIN TRIAIL AS

Ní fiú tada é. It's worthless.

16. MÚCH LÉAN LE GÁIRE

Quench sorrow with laughter. Look on the bright side. Easier said than done, of course, as it runs counter to that pessimistic streak in the Irish psyche; for example, after a few successive days of fine weather, the cry slowly arises, 'We'll surely pay for this later.'

~ BAIN TRIAIL AS ~

Múch an solas. Put out the light.

17. NÍ HÉ LÁ NA GAOITHE LÁ NA SCOLB

The windy day is not the day for thatching. *Scolb* were scollops, hazel rods for affixing the thatch. As scripture reminds us that there is a time and a season for everything, the windy day is certainly not the day for putting on a new roof. So, attune yourself to nature. Choose carefully the right time for a particular course of action.

~ BAIN TRIAIL AS ~

Ag imirt in aghaidh na gaoithe.
Playing against the wind.

18. IS TEANN GACH MADRA
AG DORAS A THÍ FÉIN

Every dog is powerful on his own doorstep – as

many a postman will aver! Ease up on the bravado. Show a little more hospitality to the visitor. Not every match will be played at home.

BAIN TRIAIL AS

Comharsa béal dorais. Next-door neighbour.

19. CUIR SÍODA AR GHABHAR AGUS IS GABHAR I gCÓNAÍ É

You can dress a goat (*gabhar*) in silk (*síoda*) but he will always (*i gcónaí*) be a goat. Accept the reality of things. Don't try to make someone/something what he/it cannot be. In a similar vein, you cannot make a silk purse from a sow's ear.

BAIN TRIAIL AS

Bíonn sé ag caint i gcónaí. He's always talking.

20. IS IOMAÍ LÁ SA CHILL ORAINN

We'll be a long time in the grave. Or, as the Connemara man said to John O'Donohue, *Beimid sínte siar cúig mhillúin bliain déag sa chré* (We'll be lying in the earth for fifteen million years). In other words, life is short. Live it to the full now. An example of mindfulness *in Éirinn fadó*. Now is the time!

BAIN TRIAIL AS

Is iomaí lá a chaith mé ann.
Many's the day I spent there.

21. IS MÓ AN FHÁILTE NÁ AN FÉASTA

The welcome is greater than the feast. We may not have much food to share with you but we'll give you a hearty welcome. It's not the size of the meal but the depth of the welcome that matters.

Tá fáilte romhat. You're welcome.

22. ARÁN MÓR IS BEAGÁN TAOIS

A big loaf of bread with little dough. Much show and little substance. When I came across this in Dinneen's dictionary, why did I automatically think of two twenty-first-century world leaders on either side of the Atlantic Ocean?

⟡ BAIN TRIAIL AS ⟡

Níl agam ach beagán. I have only a little.

23. BHÍ AN CHÚ IS AN CAT IS AN GHIORRIA AR AON URLÁR AGAM

I had a lot on my hands. An expression from Peig Sayers. Literally, I had the hound and the cat and the hare on the one floor. Imagine the mayhem the three of them would produce in pursuit of each other!

Tá cónaí orm ar an gcéad urlár.
I live on the first floor.

24. NÍ hAITHEANTAS GO hÉINTÍOS

If you want to know me, come and live with me.
You don't really get to know someone until you
live under the same roof with them. This *seanfhocal*
refers specifically to marriage, particularly in the
days when marriages were 'arranged', but it applies
equally in the general area of friendship. I think of
that wonderful television series *The Odd Couple*.

◦—◦ BAIN TRIAIL AS ◦—◦

Tá aithne agam uirthi. I know her.

25. IS GAIRE CABHAIR
DÉ NÁ AN DORAS

God's help is nearer than the door. It is here, imminent – but, of course, you have to ask for it. God, in the person of Jesus, said to us, 'Ask and you shall receive.'

⌁ BAIN TRIAIL AS ⌁

An bhfuil cabhair uait? Do you need help?

26. ANOIS NÓ GO BRÁCH!

Now or never! A rallying call. A statement of firm intent. Just imagine Elvis Presley singing, *Anois nó go brách!*

⌁ BAIN TRIAIL AS ⌁

As go brách leis. Off he went.

27. LÉIM AN CHOILIGH
   ## AR CHARN AOILIGH

The cock's step on the dungheap. A bold, imperious strut. At this time of year the days are beginning to stretch, perceptibly. My mother would refer to this as 'the cock's step on the dungheap beginning to lengthen'.

❧ BAIN TRIAIL AS ☙

D'éirigh mé le glaoch an choiligh. I rose at cockcrow.

28. IS FEARR LEATH NÁ MEATH

Half of something is better than nothing at all. Half a loaf is better than no bread. Think positively! The glass is half full rather than half empty. *Meath* means decay or failure.

❧ BAIN TRIAIL AS ☙

Leath-uair tar éis a sé. Half-past six.

29. TRÁTH LE FÍON AGUS
TRÁTH GAN BHRAON

Sometimes with wine and sometimes without a drop. Another example of *Thuas seal is thíos seal* – the rollercoaster of life. One day you're up, the next you're down.

❧ BAIN TRIAIL AS ❦

An mbeidh braon agat? Will you have a drop?

30. NÍ SCÉAL RÚIN É MÁS
FÍOR DO THRIÚR É

It's not a secret if three people know it. If it's a secret, be careful who you tell. Whatever you say, say nothing!

❧ BAIN TRIAIL AS ❦

Is fíor duit. You are right.

31. I BHFAD UAINN AN t-OLC

May evil be far from us. A wish expressed on hearing bad news. A similar expression would be, *Dia idir sinn agus an t-olc* (God between us and all harm).

⮞ BAIN TRIAIL AS ⮜

Tá an aimsir ag dul in olcas.
The weather is getting worse.

Focailín

You will surprise yourself at how much you can build your Irish vocabulary around a *focailín* (little word) like *is* – what Dinneen calls 'a verb of simple assertion'.

Is maith liom	I like
Is fearr liom	I prefer
Is trua liom	I regret
Is liom(sa) an leabhar	The book is mine
Is múinteoir í	She's a teacher
Is maith is cuimhin liom	It's well I remember
Is lag an iarracht í	It's a poor effort
Is mór an ócáid í	It's a great occasion
Is cúis áthais dom	I'm very happy
Is beag atá le rá aige	It's little he has to say

FEBRUARY

feabhra

1. NÍ THAGANN CIALL ROIMH AOIS

Sense doesn't come before age. Possibly! But then there are people like Greta Thunberg, who at the age of sixteen has awakened the world to the need for action in the face of a climate crisis. *Go raibh maith agat* (Thank you), Greta!

BAIN TRIAIL AS
Bíodh ciall agat! Have sense!

2. IS GLAS IAD NA CNOIC
I BHFAD UAINN

Faraway hills are green. Don't be misled by the initial appearance of something distant. Examine it more closely before making a decision. A similar *seanfhocal* says, *Bíonn adharca fada ar na ba thar lear* (Foreign cows have long horns).

⟶ BAIN TRIAIL AS ⟵

An ghluaiseacht ghlas. The green movement.

3. TÁ AN RATH AG RITH LEAT

Fortune is favouring you. *Rath* means good luck, success, prosperity, so when it is *ag rith leat* (running with you) you are doing well.

⟶ BAIN TRIAIL AS ⟵

Rath Dé ort. God's blessing on you.

4. IS MAITH AN SCATHÁN SÚIL CARAD

A friend's eye is a good mirror. O that we had the gift to see ourselves as others see us! There is nothing more honest than the eye of a friend (*súil carad*) that reflects us as we are rather than what we think or hope we might be.

BAIN TRIAIL AS

A chara mo chroí. O my dear friend.

5.   DÚIRT BEAN LIOM GO NDÚIRT BEAN LÉI

A woman told me that a woman told her. The evils of gossip, through which a rumour can be quickly spread and a good name destroyed. Nowadays social media replace the image of gossiping women.

BAIN TRIAIL AS

Céard a dúirt tú? What did you say?

6. NÍ FÉIDIR LEIS AN nGOBADÁN AN DÁ THRÁ A FHREASTAL

No one can serve two masters or, as St Luke put it, 'You cannot serve God and money' (Lk 16:13). The *gobadán* is the sandpiper, a little shorebird that cannot attend to the two ebb tides (*an dá thrá*), i.e. cannot work night and day. Our ancestors knew all about work–life balance!

✎ BAIN TRIAIL AS ✎

Níl an freastal go maith san ostán seo.
Service is poor in this hotel.

7. BHÍ MÉ AR MO SHÁIMHÍN SÓ

I was at my ease. Both *sámh* and *só* denote comfort and rest. Some years ago when house-hunting I found the house that I knew would offer me comfort and rest. I named the house *Sáimhín Só* – and was right!

Codladh sámh! Sleep well!

8. AN TÉ A BHUAILEANN MO MHADRA, BUAILFIDH SÉ MÉ FÉIN

He who attacks my dog will be attacking me. Man's best friend was considered a valued part of the household, so to offend or beat the dog was to offend its owner equally.

Buailfidh mé leat anocht. I'll meet you tonight.

9. DÉANANN SEILBH SÁSAMH

Possession pleases! This probably originates from a time when ownership of a property was difficult and land tenure was not guaranteed. Still relevant in modern times! I am reminded of Padraic Colum's poem 'An Old Woman of the Roads': 'O, to have a little house! To own the hearth and stool and all!'

Tá seilbh an tí agam.
I have possession of the house.

10. BEIDH LÁ EILE AG AN bPAORACH

(Mr) Power (or anyone else) will have another day. It is unclear who Mr Power was or what he did to win a second chance. Used regularly in sporting circles after a draw or a narrow defeat.

An chéad uair eile. The next time.

11. NÍ SIA GOB AN GHÉ NÁ GOB AN GHANDAIL

The goose's beak is no longer than the gander's. Six of one or half dozen of the other. A plea for equality from the farmyard?

⟿ BAIN TRIAIL AS ⟿

Tá siad gob le gob. They are neck and neck.

12. SEACHAIN AN t-OLC IS DÉAN AN MHAITH

Avoid evil and do good. There's not much arguing with that as an aspiration – but there will always be exceptions to prove the rule!

⟿ BAIN TRIAIL AS ⟿

Seachain an madra! Beware of the dog!

13. MEILEANN MUILTE DÉ GO MALL ACH MEILEANN SIAD GO MÍN

The mills of God grind slowly but they grind thoroughly. Worth saying for the alliteration alone! It may take time but everything works out in the end. Look out for *muileann* in place names; for example, *Baile an Mhuilinn* (Milltown).

⸙ BAIN TRIAIL AS ⸙

Mheilfeadh sé an croí ionat.
It would break your heart.

14. I dTOSACH NA hAICÍDE IS FUSA Í A LEIGHEAS

At the onset of the sickness it is easiest to cure. Don't dally. Tackle the problem early on and you have the best chance of resolving it.

⸙ BAIN TRIAIL AS ⸙

Níl leigheas air. It cannot be helped.

15. AN RUD IS ANNAMH IS IONTACH

What's seldom is wonderful. Whether it's a (small) lotto win, a rare victory for the local team or a surprise breakfast in bed – rejoice! Celebrate! It doesn't happen too often.

☙ BAIN TRIAIL AS ❧

Bhí an seó go hiontach. The show was wonderful.

16. NÍ DHÉANFADH AN SAOL CAPALL RÁIS D'ASAL

All the world will never make a racehorse of a donkey. Accept the limitations of the world around you. Another *seanfhocal* says with disarming logic, *An rud nach féidir, ní féidir é* (What's impossible can't be done)!

☙ BAIN TRIAIL AS ❧

Beidh saol againn. We'll have a good time.

17. NÍL LEIGHEAS AR AN nGRÁ ACH PÓSADH

Marriage is the only cure for love. *Leigheas* (cure) implies that love is a disease, so if you want the cure for that disease there is only one option. Many of the *seanfhocail* take a very cynical view of marriage, so in the interest of balance: *Más maith leat thú a cháineadh, pós* (If you want to be criticised, marry)!

⚬ BAIN TRIAIL AS ⚬

Grá mo chroí thú. I love you.

18. NA TRÍ NITHE IS GÉIRE – SÚIL CIRCE I nDIAIDH GRÁINNE, SÚIL GABHA I nDIAIDH AN TAIRNE, SÚIL MNÁ I nDIAIDH BEAN A MHIC

The three sharpest things – the eye of a hen after a grain, the eye of a blacksmith after the (horseshoe) nail, the eye of a woman after her daughter-in-law. Threes are very common in Irish literature,

often combining sharp observation with a twist of
humour or satire.

Diaidh ar ndiaidh. Gradually.

19. MOL AN ÓIGE AGUS TIOCFAIDH SÍ

Praise youth and it will respond. In times past
these were often empty words. Children were to
be seen and not heard. Curiosity would kill the
cat. Fear and repression were the order of the day.
Today we are hopefully wiser and more aware of
the child's possibility. *Moladh mór* (great praise) to
Greta Thunberg, Malala Yousafzai and their ilk.

Moladh le Dia. Praise to God.

20. DÁ FHAD AN LÁ, TAGANN OÍCHE

However long the day, night comes – whether that day be marvellous or miserable. Everything passes. All will be well.

BAIN TRIAIL AS

Go maire tú i bhfad. May you live long.

21. IS MAITH AN CHEARC NACH mBEIREANN AMUIGH

The good hen doesn't lay outside. Don't be a show-off. Stick to custom and the norm, i.e. lay your eggs in the henhouse.

BAIN TRIAIL AS

Taobh amuigh de sin. Outside of that.

22. NÍL ANN ACH SOP
IN ÁIT NA SCUAIBE

It's only a wisp (of grass) instead of a brush. It is a very poor substitute. A *sop* was a handful of hay or straw used to feed a cow or block a hole, but not much use as a *scuab* (brush).

BAIN TRIAIL AS

An scuab nua is fearr a scuabann an teach.
The new brush sweeps best.

23. SEASANN AN FHÍRINNE NUAIR
A THITEANN GACH UILE RUD

The truth stands when all else falls. However painful it may be, the truth will set your free.

BAIN TRIAIL AS

Leis an fhírinne a rá. To tell the truth.

24. GO MAIRE TÚ IS GO gCAITHE TÚ É

May you live to wear it out. A greeting to someone who is wearing a new garment. Intended as a compliment. Similar to, *Go maire tú i bhfad ná sin* (May you live much longer than that thing).

⟞ BAIN TRIAIL AS ⟝

Níl rud ar bith le caitheamh agam!
I haven't a thing to wear!

25. IS LEATH BEATHA BEAN MHAITH TÍ

A good housewife is half of life. A somewhat grudging compliment to the woman of the house. The *seanfhocail* representing the status of women *in Eirinn fadó* were anything but complimentary; for example, *Ceann gach mná a fear* (The head of every woman is her husband). But that was long ago, *buíochas le Dia* (thanks be to God)!

Beatha agus sláinte chugat! Life and health to you!

26. CUR NA FEABHRA TORADH GAN TUÍ
CUR AN MHÁRTA TUÍ AGUS TORADH
CUR AN AIBREÁIN TUÍ GAN TORADH

Sow in February, you get grain and no straw
Sow in March, you get straw and grain
Sow in April, you get straw and no grain

Another 'three' offering advice to the cereal farmer. *Toradh* means fruit or produce; in this case, grain. Plan your actions carefully.

~ BAIN TRIAIL AS ~

Toradh mo chuid oibre. The fruit of my labour.

27. GIORRAÍONN BEIRT BÓTHAR

Two people shorten the road. A journey is easier and seems shorter when shared with someone else.

≈◎ BAIN TRIAIL AS ◎≈

Tabhair do bhóthar ort! Hit the road!

28. NUAIR A BHÍONN DO LÁMH I mBÉAL AN MHADRA, TARRAING GO RÉIDH Í

When your hand is in the dog's mouth, pull it very gently. When you are in a tight corner, consider every step. Weigh your options carefully when you're in trouble.

≈◎ BAIN TRIAIL AS ◎≈

Tóg go réidh é. Take it easy.

29. NÍ THIG AN FUACHT GO dTIG AN t-EARRACH

The cold weather doesn't come until spring. Forget about winter and heed all those warnings – 'March comes in like a lion', etc.

BAIN TRIAIL AS

Tá mé préachta leis an bhfuacht.
I am famished with the cold.

Focailín

You will surprise yourself at how much you can build your Irish vocabulary around a *focailín* (little word) like:

Chomh	As
Chomh ciúin le luch	As quiet as a mouse
Chomh lag le huisce	As weak as water
Chomh glic le sionnach	As clever as a fox
Chomh milis le mil	As sweet as honey
Chomh dána le muc	As stubborn as a pig
Chomh mín le síoda	As smooth as silk
Chomh liath le broc	As grey as a badger
Chomh láidir le capall	As strong as a horse
Chomh luath le giorria	As swift as a hare
Chomh mall le seilmide	As slow as a snail

MARCH

Márta

1. IS MÓ COR A CHUIREANN LÁ MÁRTA DHE

A March day has many a twist. We're not out of the woods of winter yet, even if it is officially spring. So tread warily and expect the worst.

⤙ BAIN TRIAIL AS ⤚

Níor tharla sé in aon chor. It didn't happen at all.

2. AN TÉ A CHUIREANN SAN EARRACH, BAINFIDH SÉ SAN FHÓMHAR

He who sows in spring will reap in the autumn. Obvious practical advice for the farmer, but the thinking applies to us all. The sporting title, the academic achievement, the business success – none of them happens overnight. Harvesting of any kind takes long-term planning and commitment.

⟿ **BAIN TRIAIL AS** ⟾

Céard a bhain díot? What happened you?

3.   CHUAIGH SÉ Ó RÍ GO RÁMHAINN

He went from riches to rags. Literally, from (being a) king to (using a) spade. The descent from prosperity to penury can often be quite spectacular.

⟿ **BAIN TRIAIL AS** ⟾

Ní thabharfainn don rí é.
I wouldn't give it to the king (i.e. anybody).

4.   IS MAITH LE DIA CÚNAMH

God likes a bit of help. Being God, he doesn't *need* help, but he appreciates when we do what pleases him – offer a kindly word, help someone in trouble, be grateful!

BAIN TRIAIL AS

Le cúnamh Dé. With the help of God.

5. MAIREANN AN CROÍ ÉADROM I BHFAD

The light heart lives long. Lighten up! Be happy. Don't worry! Smile! You will live longer.

BAIN TRIAIL AS

Chomh héadrom le cleite. As light as a feather.

6. AR MHAITHE LEIS FÉIN A DHÉANANN AN CAT CRÓNÁN

The cat purrs for his own good. And why wouldn't he? If it gets him a saucer of milk, an extra treat or a little extra affection. When humans do it, it's called flattery – and it works for them too.

⊸ BAIN TRIAIL AS ⊷

Éist le crónán na mbeach.
Listen to the humming of the bees.

7. IS MAITH AN FHAIRE AN FHÓGAIRT

Forewarned is forearmed. To be warned (*fógairt*) of something in advance puts us on our guard (*faire*). *Focal faire* is a password.

⊸ BAIN TRIAIL AS ⊷

Tá an coileach ag fógairt an lae.
The cock is announcing the day (cockcrow).

8. FEILEANN SPALLAÍ DO BHALLAÍ CHOMH MAITH LE CLOCHA MÓRA

Walls require little stones as much as big ones. I once had a garden that was enclosed by a dry stone wall. When part of the wall collapsed, I tried to rebuild it. I failed a number of times until a wise neighbour explained that the secret is in remembering the *spallaí* (little stones). They are the wedges that hold the big stones together. The wall still stands. Everyone is important in any venture – even the littlest 'cogs'.

⟡ BAIN TRIAIL AS ⟡

Feileann an gúna sin duit. That dress suits you.

9. IS IAD NA MUCA CIÚINE A ITHEANN AN MHIN

It's the quiet pigs that eat the meal. Beware the quiet people – they get things done in their own way while others are busy squabbling.

Ciúnas sa chúirt! Silence in court!

10. FÁG AN BEALACH!

Get out of the way! A war cry of old, sometimes adopted as a team name by GAA clubs; for example, Castleblayney Faughs. Guaranteed to strike terror into any opponent!

Ar mo bhealach abhaile. On my way home.

11. DHÁ RÉAL, SCILLING

Six of one, a half dozen of the other. The same thing. In the (old) currency, a *scilling* (shilling/or a bob) was worth twelve pence, while the *réal* (a tanner) was worth sixpence. So, two tanners, a bob. No difference. Such a simple *seanfhocal*.

Seo í an bhliain dhá mhíle is fiche. This is the year two thousand and twenty.

12. AR SCÁTH A CHÉILE A MHAIREANN NA DAOINE

People live in the shelter of each other. When my neighbour Jo Jo Lane died in a road accident some years ago, his remains were brought to his home to be waked. Overnight a community moved quietly and efficiently into action. Traffic controls were set up on a busy road. A meadow was mowed to provide parking. A marquee was erected in the garden with chairs and tables provided. Cakes were baked, sandwiches were made. Stewards marshalled a queue of mourners. A broken family realised it lived in the shelter of a loving and supportive community.

Seo m'fhear céile. This is my husband.

13. COGADH CARAD, CAOI NAMHAD

Strife between friends is the enemy's opportunity. United we stand, divided we fall. Sort out your internal divisions and present a common front to the opposition.

BAIN TRIAIL AS

Cén chaoi a bhfuil tú? How are you?

14. NÍL LIATHADH AN TAE AICI

She has hardly anything. Literally, she hasn't the 'greying' of the tea – she hasn't even the milk for her tea. Hard times, indeed.

BAIN TRIAIL AS

Ceann liath ort. May you live long
(A grey head to you).

15. NUAIR A BHEIDH AN CAT AMUIGH, BEIDH AN LUCH AG RINCE

When the cat's away, the mice will play. Literally, the mice will dance (*ag rince*). Seize the opportunity when it arises.

BAIN TRIAIL AS

An bhfuil fonn rince ort? Are you dancing?

16. THIT AN LUG AR AN LAG AGAM

I fell apart (in dismay). Usually said when confronted by disappointing news or a hopeless situation.

BAIN TRIAIL AS

Nár laga Dia thú! More power to you (May God not weaken you)!

17. BÍONN GACH SEAN NUA
IS BÍONN GACH NUA SEAN

There is nothing new under the sun. Literally, everything old (*sean*) is new and everything new (*nua*) is old. Nothing should surprise us anymore.

BAIN TRIAIL AS

Chomh sean leis na cnoic. As old as the hills.

18. IS TÚISCE DEOCH NÁ SCÉAL

Drink precedes a story. Drink has a way of loosening the tongue. 'Did I ever tell you about the time … ?'

BAIN TRIAIL AS

An túisce a d'oscail sé a bhéal.
As soon as he opened his mouth.

19. IS FEARR LEATHBHUILÍN NÁ A BHEITH GAN ARÁN

Half a loaf is better than no bread. Make the most of what you have. Things are unlikely to improve.

BAIN TRIAIL AS

Builín breac Oíche Shamhna.
Barmbrack on Hallowe'en.

20. NÍL CÍOS, CÁS NÁ CATHÚ ORM

I haven't a worry in the world. Not a tax (*cíos*), not a regret (*cás*), not a temptation (*cathú*). A good way to be. *Tá mé ar mhuin na muice* (I'm on the pig's back).

BAIN TRIAIL AS

Ná lig sinn i gcathú. Lead us not into temptation.

21. IS LEOR Ó DHUINE A DHÍCHEALL

One's best is enough. The common cry from today's team managers and business leaders is 'Give me your best', or 'your almighty best' as a John B. Keane character might say. And if the players/workers do, no complaints. *Is leor sin* (That's enough).

⟶ BAIN TRIAIL AS ⟵

Déan do dhícheall. Do your best.

22. NÍ BHÍONN AN RATH ACH MAR A mBÍONN AN SMACHT

Success demands discipline. Another slogan beloved of team managers. 'Our discipline was poor. You can't expect to win, giving away penalties/ frees like that.'

⟶ BAIN TRIAIL AS ⟵

Tá an tír faoi smacht an airm.
The country is under the control of the army.

23. NUAIR A BHUAILEANN AN CRÚ AR AN TAIRNE

When the horseshoe comes down on the nail. When it comes right down to it. When push comes to shove. The reference is to shoeing a horse – that exact moment when the shoe (*crú*) meets the nail (*tairne*).

BAIN TRIAIL AS

Seachain an tairne! Watch out for the nail!

24. IS TREISE DIA NÁ DÓCHAS

God is stronger than hope. Far better to put your trust in God than to be merely hopeful about something.

BAIN TRIAIL AS

Sé mo dhóchas. I hope very much.

25. TÁ SIN AG BAINT NA TUA AS LÁIMH AN tSAOIR

That's all pretence. Literally, taking the axe (*tua*) out of the craftsman's (*saor*) hand. A common enough phenomenon where 'experts' arise and make pronouncements, pretending they have superior knowledge over all others.

⌒ BAIN TRIAIL AS ⌒

Suigh lámh liom. Sit beside me.

26. LUÍ LE hUAIN AGUS ÉIRÍ LE hÉIN

Early to bed and early to rise
Makes a man healthy and wealthy and wise.
Literally, to bed with the lambs and rise with the birds. Practical advice for a healthy lifestyle.

⌒ BAIN TRIAIL AS ⌒

An luíonn an áit seo leat? Do you like this place?

27. BRISEANN AN DÚCHAS TRÍ SHÚILE AN CHAIT

True nature cannot be suppressed. Literally, nature breaks out through the eyes of the cat. He will chase and catch the mice. There are many variants on this *seanfhocal*; for example, *Tiocfaidh an dúchas trí na crúba is leanfaidh an chú an giorria* (Nature will come through the paws and the hound will follow the hare). It applies equally to humans – as we are, so shall we ultimately act. Nature outstrips nurture.

⟿ BAIN TRIAIL AS ⟽

Is í seo m'áit dhúchais. This is my native place.

28. NÍ FADA ÓNA GHOL A GHÁIRE

Tears can quickly change to laughter. Literally, his tears are not far from his laughter. *Thuas seal, thíos seal!*

Gáire os ard. Laughing out loud. You can use GOA instead of LOL in your text messages.

29. NÍ CHUIMHNÍTEAR AR AN ARÁN A ITEAR

Eaten bread is soon forgotten. Time passes. How quickly we forget!

Beidh cuimhne go deo agam air.
I'll always remember him.

30. AN TÉ A BHÍONN FIAL, ROINNEANN DIA LEIS

God rewards the generous person. Literally, God shares (*roinneann*) with the generous (*fial*) one. Be kind to others and God will be kind to you.

Tá roinnt airgid agam. I have some money.

31. THUG SÉ ÍDE NA MUC IS NA MADRAÍ DOM

He gave me an awful time. Literally, he treated me like a pig or a dog. He tore strips off me. He gave me 'dog's abuse'. Definitely not the mark of a generous person (*duine fial*).

⇜ BAIN TRIAIL AS ⇝

Íde béil. A telling-off.

Focailín

You will surprise yourself at how much you can build your Irish vocabulary around a *focailín* (little word) like:

Seo	This
Seo dhuit	Here you are (This is for you)
Seo mo theach	This is my house
Seo linn	Here we go
Seo mar a tharla	This is how it happened
Mar seo	Like this
An Satharn seo chugainn	This coming Saturday
Roimhe seo	Before this
As seo amach	From this on
Go dtí seo	Before this/up to now
Seo é	This is it

APRIL

Aibreán

1. AMADÁN, AMADÁN, AN CHÉAD LÁ d'AIBREÁN

April Fool! Literally, Fool! Fool! The first day of April. A nonsense rhyme for the day that's in it.

⟶ BAIN TRIAIL AS ⟵

Lá breithe sona duit. Happy birthday to you.

2. TÁ MÉ IM' OISÍN I nDIAIDH NA FÉINNE

I'm a lost soul, a sole survivor. When Oisín returned from Tír na nÓg he found that all his companions in the Fianna (*an Fhiann*) were long dead.

Tháinig siad i ndiaidh a chéile.
They came one after the other.

3. AN MADRA RUA I mBUN NA gCEARC

A ridiculous decision. Literally, the fox in charge of the hens. Turkeys voting for Christmas.

∽◦ BAIN TRIAIL AS ◦∽

Cé tá i mbun oibre anseo?
Who is in charge (of work) here?

4. SÉ AN t-ÉADACH AN DUINE

Clothes maketh the man – or woman. A compliment to the well-dressed person.

∽◦ BAIN TRIAIL AS ◦∽

Mo chuid éadaigh. My clothes.

5. IS FEARR FOCAL SA CHÚIRT NÁ PUNT SA SPARÁN

A word in court is better than a pound in the purse. Money isn't always the answer. The testimony of a friend is priceless.

Focal i do chluas. A word in your ear.

6. MAIREANN AN CHRAOBH AR AN bhFÁL ACH NÍ MHAIREANN AN LÁMH A CHUIR

Nature outlives us all. Literally, the branch lives on in the hedge but the hand that planted it is gone. In the grounds of Birr Castle, Co. Offaly, there is a project called the Giant's Grove – a plantation of giant redwood trees. One of them is sponsored by me and dedicated to my family. When I am long gone from this earth, this majestic tree will still flourish and help the environment.

Rug sé an chraobh leis. He won the prize (garland).

7. MÚINEANN GÁ SEIFT

Necessity is the mother of invention. When there is a need (*gá*) for something, that need will produce a plan (*seift*).

Níl aon ghá leis sin. There's no need for that.

8. NUAIR A BHÍONN AN BRAON ISTIGH, BÍONN AN CHIALL AMUIGH

Beware the dangers of alcohol. Literally, when the 'drop' is within, the sense is without. If you persist with the drink, you'll make a fool of yourself.

Istigh cois tine nó amuigh faoin spéir. Inside by the
fire or outside beneath the sky.

9.   NÍL SÉ ANN BUÍ, BÁN NÁ DUBH

It's not there at all, at all. Literally, it's not there
yellow, white or black. Said when something has
totally disappeared.

Bhí mé ag obair ó dhubh go dubh.
I was working all day long (from dark to dark).

10.   FILLEANN AN FEALL
    AR AN bhFEALLAIRE

Curses come home to roost. Literally, evil (*feall*)
returns to the evildoer (*feallaire*). A nice piece of
alliteration.

Fill abhaile liom. Come home with me.

11. IS CEIRÍN GACH CRÉACHT AN FHOIGHNE

Patience (*foighne*) heals all wounds (*créacht*). *Ceirín* is a plaster or poultice. No matter how deeply you have been hurt, be patient. Time is a great healer.

Bíodh foighne agat. Be patient.

12. IS UALACH ÉADROM Í AN FHOGHLAIM ACH IS ÁBHAR ACHRAINN Í GO MINIC

Learning is a light burden but it can also cause disputes. A little learning can be a dangerous thing.

Ualach mic na leisce. The lazy man's load.

13. NÍ THAGANN RITH MAITH DON EACH I gCÓNAÍ

There is no such thing as a racing certainty – despite what you may have been told! Literally, the horse (*each*) doesn't always get a good run. Misfortune can happen. As another *seanfhocal* says, *Is minic nach é an capall is fearr a thógann an rás* (The best horse doesn't always win the race).

Níl sé ach rith circe ón áit seo. It's only a hen's run (short distance) from here.

14. IS MAITH É DIA Ó INNIU GO dTÍ AMÁRACH

God is good from day to day. Literally, God is good from today to tomorrow. Simply, God is good. Fear not. He will provide.

— BAIN TRIAIL AS —

Inniu an Satharn. Amárach an Domhnach. Today is Saturday. Tomorrow is Sunday.

15. I nDOMHAN NA nDALL IS RÍ FEAR AONSÚILEACH

Among the blind, the one-eyed man is king. Play to your strength. If you have an advantage, make use of it.

— BAIN TRIAIL AS —

Tá cáil air ar fud an domhain.
He is famous all over the world.

16. IS FEARR 'SEO' AMHÁIN NÁ DHÁ 'GHEOBHAIDH TÚ'

A bird in the hand is worth two in the bush. Literally, one 'Here you are' is better than two 'You will get'. Promises, promises! Settle for what you can have now.

 BAIN TRIAIL AS

Tá an seic sa phost. Gheobhaidh tú é amárach! The cheque is in the post. You'll get it tomorrow!

17. NÍ THUIGTEAR FEIDHM AN TOBAIR GO dTÉANN SÉ I dTRÁ

You never miss the water till the well runs dry. Literally, the function of the well (*feidhm an tobair*) is not recognised until it runs dry. Never take things for granted.

Bain feidhm as an eolas sin.
Make use of that knowledge.

18. MÉADAÍONN TAITHÍ TOIL

Experience (*taithí*) increases desire (*toil*). The more we use something, the more we like it and want more. The power of addiction.

⚬❖ BAIN TRIAIL AS ❖⚬

Tá sean-taithí agam air. I am well used to it.

19. TADHG AN DÁ THAOBH

Teddy two-sides. A double dealer, not to be trusted. *Ná bí i do Thadhg an dá thaobh* (Don't sit on both sides of the fence). Dinneen has a wonderful name for the 'man in the moon' – *Tadhg na Scuab*!

Ó mo thaobh féin de. From my point of view.

20. NÍL BUN NÁ BARR LEIS AN SCÉAL SIN

That story is total nonsense. Literally, there is neither head (*barr*) nor tail (*bun*) to that story. It's all over the place!

⚬ BAIN TRIAIL AS ⚬

Bhí an cluiche sin thar barr.
That game was excellent.

21. GLAC LEIS AN SAOL MAR ATÁ SÉ

Take the world as you find it. Sometimes, it's best to take things as they are. You can't change everything!

Is olc an saol é. It's a wicked old world.

22. IS BUAN FEAR INA DHÚTHAIGH FÉIN

A man is long-lived in his own country. Even when he is physically gone, his memory lives on, so respect the local hero.

⟆ BAIN TRIAIL AS ⟅

Molann gach éinne a dhúthaigh féin.
Everyone praises his own country.

23. IS MAOL GUALA GAN BHRÁTHAIR

One shoulder (*guala*) is not enough. Without the help of a brother or kinsman (*bráthair*) one is defenceless. A variation of *Ní neart go cur le chéile* (United we stand).

Guala ar ghualainn. Shoulder to shoulder.

24. IS MAITH AN t-IOMÁNAÍ AN TÉ A BHÍONN AR AN gCLAÍ

The hurler on the ditch knows best. A sardonic remark. The person who is not involved in the contest thinks he knows best. We have all met the hurler on the ditch – the one who has a remedy for all ills.

An t-iománaí is fearr sa tír.
The best hurler in the country.

25. BÉARFAIDH BÓ ÉIGIN LAO ÉIGIN LÁ ÉIGIN

Something good will happen. Literally, someday (*lá éigin*) some cow (*bó*) will give birth to some calf (*lao*). The mantra of an optimist. Always look on the bright side!

Duine éigin eile. Somebody else.

26. OBAIR GAN CHRÍOCH, OBAIR NA MNÁ TÍ

A housewife's work is without end. An English variation of this is, 'A man's work is from sun to sun but a woman's work is never done.'

Rinne sé obair na gcapall.
He did the heavy work (the horses' work).

27. IS FEARR RITH MAITH
NÁ DROCH-SHEASAMH

Discretion is the better part of valour. Literally, a
good retreat is better than a bad stand. Sometimes
the wisest option is to step back and live to fight
another day.

⤙ BAIN TRIAIL AS ⤚

Ní féidir liom é a sheasamh. I can't stand it.

28. NÍL MISNEACH AN CHAIT AGAT

You haven't the courage of a cat. You're a total
coward. An equivalent would be *Níl croí luiche
ionat* (You haven't the heart of a mouse).

⤙ BAIN TRIAIL AS ⤚

Muscail do mhisneach!
Summon (wake up) your courage!

29. IS FEARR CINN NÁ CEANN –
MUNA MBEADH IONTU ACH
DHÁ CHEANN SEAN-CHAORACH

Two heads (*cinn*) are better than one (*ceann*). The *seanfhocail* adds the sting: even if they are only two old sheepheads (*cheann sean-chaorach*). Take account of other opinions, even if they are of doubtful origin.

➤ BAIN TRIAIL AS ☞

Ceann ar cheann. One by one.

30. TÁ GACH DUINE LÁCH GO
dTÉANN AN BHÓ INA GHARRAÍ

Everyone is obliging until the cow enters their garden. An old saying that is as relevant as ever today. Not in my back yard! In olden days a garden was precious, supplying a family's vegetables, so a stray cow breaking into it was a major disaster.

➤ BAIN TRIAIL AS ☞

Fear lách is ea é. He's an obliging man.

Focailín

You will surprise yourself at how much you can build your Irish vocabulary around a *focailín* (little word) like:

Sin	That
Sin sin	That's that!
Sin é	That's it
Cad é sin	What's that?
Is leor sin	That's enough
Ina dhiaidh sin	After that
Leis sin	With that
As sin amach	From that on
An oiread sin	That much
Déanfaidh sin an gnó	That will do
D'imigh sin is tháinig seo	That went and this came (Life went on)

MAY

bealtaine

1. IS FEARR AN tSLÁINTE NÁ NA TÁINTE

Health is better than wealth. No arguing with that! *Táinte* means flock and herds – and, therefore, wealth. Nice wordplay. *Táin* can also mean a raid as in *Táin Bó Cuaille*, the epic story of the Brown Bull of Cooley.

↬ BAIN TRIAIL AS ↫

Na táinte póg! Millions of kisses!

2. TÁ MÉ AG OBAIR DOMHNACH IS DÁLACH

I am working all hours. Literally, I am working Sundays and weekdays. A need for some work–life balance here! *Domhnach* can also mean a church, as in the place name *Domhnach Mór* (Donaghmore).

━◦◦ BAIN TRIAIL AS ◦◦━

Beidh mé leat Dé Domhnaigh.
I'll be with you on Sunday.

3. NA TRÍ hANACRAÍ MÓRA – CÚNGRACH TÍ, CÚNGRACH BÍ, CÚNGRACH CROÍ

The three great afflictions (*anacraí*) – a narrow house, scant food and a mean heart. Another example of a 'three'. Serious afflictions, indeed.

━◦◦ BAIN TRIAIL AS ◦◦━

In am an bhia a rugadh tú! You were born at mealtime! Said to someone who habitually calls at mealtime.

4. LÁ MILLTE NA MÓNA, LÁ FÓMHAIR AN CHABÁISTE

The day that ruins the turf will grow the cabbage. The rain ruins the turf but grows the cabbage. There's an upside to everything. What's bad news for some is good news for others.

⟶ BAIN TRIAIL AS ⟵

Cuir fód móna ar an tine.
Put a sod of turf on the fire.

5. NÍL LEIGHEAS AR AN gCATHÚ ACH É A MHARÚ LE FOIGHNE

Bear your trials with patience. Literally, the only cure for a trial or sorrow is to kill it with patience.

⟶ BAIN TRIAIL AS ⟵

Marbh le tae is marbh gan é. Killed with (drinking) the tea and killed without it.

6. AN TÉ NACH mBEIREANN AR A GHNÓ, BEIREANN AN GNÓ AIR

If you don't get on top of your job, the job will get on top of you. A plea for job satisfaction. If you don't like it, leave it.

BAIN TRIAIL AS

Déanfaidh sin an gnó. That will do (the business).

7. (NÓ) NÍ LÁ GO MAIDIN É

(Either) I am greatly mistaken. Literally it is not daytime. As in, *Chonaic mé Seán nó ní lá go maidin é* (I saw Sean unless I am greatly mistaken).

BAIN TRIAIL AS

Tá sé ina lá. The day has dawned.

8. IS FEARR AN MHAITH ATÁ NÁ AN DÁ MHAITH DO BHÍ

Carpe diem! Seize the opportunity! Literally, the present good is better than two goods that were. The present good is the most valued.

✺ BAIN TRIAIL AS ✺

Maith go leor. Good enough.

9. BEIREANN AN MHOILL AN BARR LÉI

The more haste, the less speed. Literally, delay wins the day. *Barr* in this case means advantage or superiority.

✺ BAIN TRIAIL AS ✺

Beidh mé ann gan mhoill.
I'll be there straight away (without delay).

10. NÍOR ORDAIGH DIA BÉAL GAN BHIA

God has made food for all. He is the good provider. Literally, God never made a mouth that didn't have food.

⟋ BAIN TRIAIL AS ⟍

D'ordaigh sé dom é a dhéanamh.
He ordered me to do it.

11. AN SCUAB NUA IS FEARR A SCUABANN AN TEACH

A new broom sweeps clean. Literally, a new broom (*scuab*) sweeps the house best. Sometimes it's best to change personnel or start again from scratch.

⟋ BAIN TRIAIL AS ⟍

Scuab leat! Be off with you! Get lost!

12. IS FEARR SÚIL LE GLAS NÁ SÚIL LE hUAIGH

The grave comes to us all. Literally, better to hope (*súil*) for the prison (*glas*) than for the grave (*uaigh*). You can be released from one, but the other is final.

~ BAIN TRIAIL AS ~

Tá súil agam go mbeidh tú ann.
I hope you'll be there.

13. IDIR DHÁ THINE LAE BEALTAINE

In a dilemma. A reference to the practice of driving cattle between (*idir*) two fires on the first day of May (*lá Bealtaine*) with a view to their protection. When a difficult decision has to be made. Similar to *idir dhá chomhairle* (Between two advices).

~ BAIN TRIAIL AS ~

Tine chnámh Oíche Shamhna.
A Hallowe'en bonfire.

14. NÍ TROIMIDE AN LOCH AN LACHA

It's an easily borne matter. Literally, the lake (*loch*) is no heavier for the duck (*lacha*) that is swimming on it! It's of no great consequence. No big deal!

◦—◦ BAIN TRIAIL AS ◦—◦

Is breá liom Dónall Lacha. I like Donald Duck.

15. NÍ RAIBH BEO NÁ CEO ANN

There was nothing to be seen. Literally, there wasn't a living person (*beo*) or fog (*ceo*) there. Move along! Nothing to be seen here.

◦—◦ BAIN TRIAIL AS ◦—◦

Beo ó Pháirc an Chrócaigh! Live from Croke Park!

16. CEART DOM, CEART DUIT

Fair play all round. Literally, what's right (*ceart*) for me is right for you. *Cothrom na Féinne* (the equality of the Fianna) is another expression for fair play.

BAIN TRIAIL AS

Tá an ceart agat! You are right!

17. DHÉANFADH SÉ CAT IS DHÁ EIREABALL

He would work wonders. Literally, he would make a cat with two tails! A most wonderful invention, indeed.

BAIN TRIAIL AS

Eireaball an lae. The close of the day.

18. GACH DALTA MAR A n-OILTEAR

The child is father to the man. Literally, each young person (*dalta*) as he is trained. Early formation proves durable. There are many variations on this theme; for example, *Nuair a chruann an tslat, is deacair í a lúbadh* (As the rod hardens, it's difficult to bend it), a reference to sally rods in the weaving of baskets.

∼◦ BAIN TRIAIL AS ◦∼

Is fearr an oiliúint ná an t-oideachas. Upbringing (*oiliúint*) counts for more than education.

19. MÁ TÁ DO DHÍOL SA CHAIPÍN, CAITH É

If the cap fits, wear it. *Díol* means satisfaction or, simply, enough. Choose what really appeals to you. Can also be said with sarcasm, of course.

Chaith mé an lá cois trá.
I spent the day at the seaside.

20. IS FUAR AN RUD É CLÚ GAN CHARA

Fame without friendship is a cold place. We have read the novel or seen the movie about the person who 'has it all' but at heart is lonely and isolated and yearns for a friend.

Tá clú uirthi ar fud na tíre.
She is famous all over the country.

21. GALAR GAN NÁIRE GRÁ AGUS TART ACH BUANN AN TOCHAS AIR

Love and thirst (*tart*) are diseases that know no shame but the itch (*tochas*) beats all! There's nothing worse than having an itch you can't scratch.

Dinneen has the wonderful expression, *Tochas agus díth ingne, eascaine Chromail* (Cromwell's curse, to have an itch and no nail [to scratch it]). Poor old Cromwell got the blame for everything.

◦◦◦ BAIN TRIAIL AS ◦◦◦

Mo náire thú! I'm ashamed of you.

22. IS FEARR SEANFHIACHA NÁ SEANFHALTA

Old debts are preferable to old grudges. Debts can be wiped out or forgotten in time but grudges tend to last.

◦◦◦ BAIN TRIAIL AS ◦◦◦

Tá sé i bhfiacha. He is in debt.

23. NÍL AON TINTEÁN MAR DO THINTEÁN FÉIN

There is no place like home. Probably one of the best known of the *seanfhocail*. This is more specific than its English counterpart: literally, there is no hearth (*tinteán*) like your own hearth. In pre-television days, the fireplace was the heart and focus of the home, where visitors were welcomed, stories were exchanged and families gathered. It was where cooking was done and was often the source of light as well as heat.

⟿ BAIN TRIAIL AS ⟿

Suigh anseo cois tine. Sit here by the fire.

24. TRÍ SHÓLÁS AN tSEANDUINE – TINE, TAE AGUS TOBAC

The old person's three comforts – fire, tea and tobacco. Simple pleasures in olden days, even if one of them was injurious to health, as we now know.

Ní bhíonn sólás gan dólás.
Comfort is not without sorrow. (Peig Sayers)

25. IS LIA GACH OTHAR TAR ÉIS A LEIGHIS

Every patient (*othar*) is a physician (*lia*) after his cure – and if allowed, will bore you with the details. Shall I tell you about my operation? A successful experience often induces boastfulness.

Cuir glaoch ar an otharcharr. Ring the ambulance.

26. NÍ BHEIDH A LEITHÉID ARÍS ANN

We'll not see his like again. Adapted from the immortal closing lines of Tomás Ó Criomhthain's *An t-Oileánach – Ní bheidh ár leithéidí arís ann –*

and worn almost to a cliché from its frequent use in tributes and eulogies.

A leithéid de chluiche! What a game!

27. NÍ RAIBH AN DARA SUÍ SA BHUAILE AIGE

He had no alternative. Literally, he hadn't a second sitting in the booley (a milking place for cattle). Listen to how a *tráchtaire* (commentator) like Brian Tyers might use it – *Ní raibh an dara suí sa bhuaile aige ach an liathróid a ghlanadh thar an líne* (He had no option but to clear the ball over the line). Pressurised situations bring reduced options.

Bíonn sé anseo gach dara lá.
He's here every second day.

28. IS MAITH AN t-ANLANN AN t-OCRAS

Hunger is a good sauce. As your grandmother might say, 'If you're hungry enough, you'll eat it.' Or as my own father used say, in chiding us for leaving a crust on the plate, 'You'll follow a crow for that someday!'

⟿ **BAIN TRIAIL AS** ⟾

Tá ocras mór orm. I'm starving.

29. IS FEARR RÉAL INNIU NÁ SCILLING AMÁRACH

A bird in the hand is worth two in the bush. A *réal* (sixpence) might only be half a *scilling* (shilling) but better the reality of the former in your hand today than the prospect of the latter tomorrow. Take what's going now.

⟿ **BAIN TRIAIL AS** ⟾

An inniu an Aoine? Ní hea. Amárach an Aoine.
Is today Friday? No. Tomorrow is Friday.

30. TUIGEANN TADHG TAIDHGÍN

It takes one to know one. One rogue understands another. Concise and alliterative!

◦ BAIN TRIAIL AS ◦

Ní thuigim focal uait.
I don't understand a word you say.

31. TÁ CAINT SAOR AGUS AIRGEAD AR THOBAC

Talk is cheap but tobacco must be paid for – as every government budget reminds us. Talk is probably the only remaining life's pleasure that doesn't cost us but be careful! It could eventually cost you in a court of law!

◦ BAIN TRIAIL AS ◦

Bhí sé saor go leor. It was cheap enough.

Focailín

You will surprise yourself at how much you can build your Irish vocabulary around a *focailín* (little word) like:

Mar	As/Like
Mar seo	Like this
Mar sin	Like that
Mar atá/a bhí	As it is/was
Mar sin féin	Even so
Mar a leanas	As follows
Mar is cóir	As is proper
Mar dhea	What seems to be/ 'As if'
Mar shampla	For example
Fé/Faoi mar	Just as
Mar a deirtear	As they say

JUNE
Meitheamh

1. IS MAITH AN CAIRDE LÁ FADA SAMHRAIDH

A long summer's day is good 'credit'. A sunny day in June offers a welcome respite. Daylight extends to its maximum in June. Enjoy. Summer is really here.

❧ BAIN TRIAIL AS ❧

Tagann gach maith le cairde.
Time brings every blessing.

2. AITHNÍTEAR CARA I gCRUATAN

A friend in need is a friend indeed. Literally, a friend is recognised in hard times. There are many variations on this theme. *Ní easpa go díth carad* (There is no need like the lack of a friend).

⟶ BAIN TRIAIL AS ⟵

Tá cruatan mór sa tSiria.
There is great hardship in Syria.

3. TÁ AN LEITE AR FUD NA MIAS

Another fine mess – in the immortal words of Oliver Hardy. Literally, the porridge (*leite*) is (spilled) all over the dishes. Something has gone horribly wrong.

⟶ BAIN TRIAIL AS ⟵

Thit sneachta ar fud na tíre.
Snow fell all over the country.

4.   IS FEARR ÉIRÍ MOCH NA SUÍ MALL

Early to bed and early to rise makes one healthy and wealthy and wise. Not sure about the 'wealthy' part, although our former taoiseach Leo Varadkar favours early risers who help drive our economy. Literally, early rising is better than late sitting.

⤠ BAIN TRIAIL AS ⤟

Bí ann – moch nó mall. Be there – early or late.

5.   TROID NA mBÓ MAOL A BHÍ ANN

It was a harmless event. Literally, it was a fight between hornless (*maol*) cows (who could do little damage to each other). Much ado about nothing. In sporting circles, it might describe a 'friendly' or meaningless end-of-season match.

⤠ BAIN TRIAIL AS ⤟

Is fearr maol ná a bheith gan cheann ach níl ann ach sin. Better to be bald than headless.

6. TÁ SLÁINTE AN BHRADÁIN AIGE

He's in the best of health. Literally, he has the health of a salmon. Probably because of its endurance in returning to spawning grounds, the salmon is associated with robust health.

↪ BAIN TRIAIL AS ↩

A toast!
Sláinte na bhfear is go maire na mná go deo.
A health to the men and long live the women.

7. SCEITHEANN AN FÍON FÍRINNE

Wine (*fíon*) reveals the truth (*fírinne*). Drink loosens the tongue and the truth will out when caught off guard. One of many *seanfhocail* that demonise drink.

↪ BAIN TRIAIL AS ↩

Fíon geal, le do thoil. White wine, please.

8. LEIGHEAS GACH BRÓN COMHRÁ

Talking heals sorrow. Good practical advice for the grieving. It's good to talk!

◦◦ BAIN TRIAIL AS ◦◦

Ábhár mór chómhrá a bhí ann.
It was a great topic for conversation.

9. AN CHÉAD BHLIAIN, BLIAIN NA bPÓG
AN DARA BLIAIN, BLIAIN NA nDORN

The first year, it's kisses non-stop. The second year, the gloves are off. A harshly cynical view of marriage, quite typical of the attitude to marriage in many *seanfhocail. Bliain na ndorn* literally means the year of the fists, so the honeymoon (*mí na meala*) is definitely over. In the same vein, *Ón lá a bpósfaidh tú, beidh do chroí i do bhéal agus do lámh i do phóca* (From the day you marry, your heart will be in your mouth and your hand in your pocket).

Thóg sé dorn airgid as a phóca.
He took a fistful of money from his pocket.

10. NÍ NEART GO CUR LE CHÉILE

United we stand! Coming together makes us strong (*neart*). A much-quoted *seanfhocal* for rallying teams and communities.

Níl neart agam air. I cannot help it.

11. SÚIL LE CÚITEAMH A MHILLEAS AN CEARRBHACH

The hope (*súil*) of winning back destroys the gambler (*cearrbhach*). A stern warning to the losing gambler. Just one more hand of cards or one more bet is never going to recoup (*cúiteamh*) your losses. Quit now! Card-playing was a very popular pastime among our ancestors.

BAIN TRIAIL AS

Bhí súil agam le lá breá ach mhill an bháisteach é.
I was looking forward to a good day
but the rain ruined it.

12. IS FEARR PAISTE NÁ POLL ACH NÍL ANN ACH SIN

A patch is better than a hole, but that's the best that can be said about it. A repaired piece of clothing may look respectable, but it is still only a patch.

BAIN TRIAIL AS

Tá poll sa bhuicéad, a Anraí!
There's a hole in the bucket, dear Henry!

Bhuel, deisigh é, a Eilís! Well fix it, dear Liza!

13. MAIR, A CHAPAILL AGUS GHEOBHAIR FÉAR

Live, horse and you'll get grass. You will be rewarded according to the standards you set. Aim high and you'll do well.

⟋☙ BAIN TRIAIL AS ☙⟍

Go maire tú an céad. May you live to be a hundred.

14. NÍ CATHAIR MAR A TUAIRISC Í

It's not all it's cracked up to be. Literally, it's not the city or mansion (*cathair*) it was reported to be. An expression of disappointment in a person or event.

⟋☙ BAIN TRIAIL AS ☙⟍

Bhí sé ag cur do thuairisce.
He was asking about you.

15. NÁ DÉAN 'PAIDIR CHAPAILL' DE

Don't make an endless rigmarole of it. Literally, don't make a 'horse's prayer' of it. A reference to a plough horse stumbling on his knees (as if in prayer) and spending a long time thus. Get to the point! Another version: *Tá sé ina phaidir eadair agat* (You have made a right rigmarole of it).

⤙ BAIN TRIAIL AS ⤚

Abair paidir ar mo shon. Say a prayer for me.

16. NÍL TÁSC NÁ TUAIRISC AIR

There's no trace of him. *Tásc* and *tuairisc* have the same meaning – an account or report.

⤙ BAIN TRIAIL AS ⤚

Seo tuairisc ó Bhéal Feirste.
Here's a report from Belfast.

17. NÍ BHÍONN IN AON RUD ACH SEAL

Everything passes. Literally, nothing lasts but for a while (*seal*). A nine-day wonder – or less!

BAIN TRIAIL AS

Chaith mé seal dem' shaol thar lear.
I spent a part of my life abroad.

18. AN RUD NACH BINN LE DUINE, NÍ CHLOISEANN SÉ É

We only hear what we want to hear. Literally, a person doesn't hear what is not pleasant (*binn*) to his ears.

BAIN TRIAIL AS

Tá guth binn agat. You have a sweet voice.

19. GO n-ITHE AN CAT THÚ IS GO n-ITHE AN DIABHAL AN CAT

May the cat eat you and may the devil eat the cat. While the *seanfhocail* abound in blessings (*beannachtaí*), there are plenty of curses (*mallachtaí*) too – and this is a fairly vicious example!

⟶ BAIN TRIAIL AS ⟵

An mbeidh rud le n-ithe agat?
Will you have something to eat?

20. AN RUD A CHÍONN AN LEANBH IS É A NÍONN AN LEANBH

The child does what the child sees. Be careful of the example you give to little ones. They are watching you closely.

⟶ BAIN TRIAIL AS ⟵

Chím gach rud go soiléir anois.
I see everything clearly now.

21. TÁ ÉISTEACHT NA MUICE BRADAÍ AIGE

He has sharp hearing. Literally, he has the hearing (*éisteacht*) of a thieving pig (*muc bhradach*). It might further be said, *D'aireodh sé an féar ag fás* (He would hear the grass growing)!

⤍ BAIN TRIAIL AS ⤎

Níl tú ag éisteacht liom. You're not listening to me.

22. AITHNÍONN CIARÓG CIARÓG EILE

It takes one to know one. Literally, one beetle recognises another. People of similar minds will recognise each other.

⤍ BAIN TRIAIL AS ⤎

Aithním go bhfuil díomá ort.
I can see you're disappointed.

23. TÁ DIA LÁIDIR IS MÁTHAIR MHAITH AIGE

God is good (strong) and he has a good mother. A simple expression of trust in the providence of God, usually in a time of need or danger. Not only that, but the same God has a merciful mother at his side.

⟡ BAIN TRIAIL AS ⟡

Tá an lámh láidir aige. He has the upper hand.

24. CÚL LE GAOTH AND AGHAIDH LE TEAS

Back to the wind and face to the heat (sun). The ideal site for a house but also a good recommendation for the game of life – get the wind behind your back, face into the sun and you'll be grand!

⟡ BAIN TRIAIL AS ⟡

Thug mé aghaidh ar an mbaile. I set out for the town.

25. TREABH AN t-IOMAIRE ATÁ ROMHAT

Do what needs to be done now. Literally, plough the furrow (*iomaire*) that's before you. Attend to present duties.

↬ BAIN TRIAIL AS ↫

Táim ag treabhadh liom.
I am ploughing away/doing my best.

26. NÍ BHÍONN SÓ GAN ANÓ

There is no pleasure without pain. Peig Sayers put it like this: *Ní bhíonn an sólás gan an dólás á choimhdeacht.* Comfort is usually accompanied by discomfort.

↬ BAIN TRIAIL AS ↫

Ní bhíonn deatach gan tine.
There's no smoke without fire.

27. FUAIR SÉ AN POTA IS AN MÁLA

He got more than he was entitled to. Literally, he got the pot and the bag (and whatever they contained!). He did pretty well.

⤟ BAIN TRIAIL AS ⤞

Tá lán an mhála aige. He has the full bag, i.e. plenty. (Often anglicised to lawn-a-wall-ye.)

28. IS DÁNA BEAN NÁ MUC AGUS IS DÁNA MUC NÁ AN DIABHAL

A woman is more stubborn than a pig and a pig is more stubborn than the devil. Not true, of course, but included here as an example of the low status of women in the *seanfhocail*. And hard on the pig too – in reality a clean and intelligent animal. I once made a radio documentary – *Pighomage* – to make up for the bad press the pig gets.

Bhí sé ag obair ar nós an diabhail.
He was working like the devil, i.e. very intensely.

29. CAPALL NA hOIBRE AN BIA

Food is the energy that drives us. Literally, food is
the workhorse. My late wife used to say of a certain
person, 'If you want him to work, feed him first.'
She knew me so well. *Ní beo gan bia sinn* (Food is
life).

Is bia agus is deoch dó é. It's food and drink to him.
Food and drink are his greatest pleasure.

30. NÁ BAC LE MAC AN BHACAIGH IS NÍ BHACFAIDH MAC AN BHACAIGH LEAT

Be careful about starting a row or 'casting the first stone'. Literally, don't bother with the beggar man's son (*mac an bhacaigh*) and he won't bother you. Best known as a tongue-twister (say it quickly three times!) but a true *seanfhocal* also.

❧ BAIN TRIAIL AS ❧

Ná bac le tobac! Stay away from tobacco!

Focailín

You will surprise yourself at how much you can build your Irish vocabulary around a *focailín* (little word) like:

Gan	Without
Gan dabht	Without a doubt
Gan mhoill	Without delay
Gan chead	Without permission
Gan airgead	Penniless
Gan é sin a rá	Without saying that
Gan chúis	Without reason
Gan aithne gan urlabhra	Unconscious
Gan chara	Friendless
Gan tigh gan treabh	Homeless/Displaced
Gan mhaith	Useless

JULY

กรกฎาคม

1. TIOCFAIDH AN LÁ FÓS A mBEIDH
   GNÓ AG AN mBÓ DÁ hEIREABALL

The day will come when the cow will have use for her tail (*eireaball*). Said to be a sign of hot weather, when the tail would definitely be useful. Everything has its use eventually.

~ BAIN TRIAIL AS ~

Cruinniú gnó ar siúl. Business meeting in progress.

2. GHOIDFEADH SÉ AN
   CHROS DEN ASAL

He's an out-and-out thief or rogue. Literally, he would steal the 'cross' from an ass's back.

Ná déan goid! Thou shalt not steal!

3. NÍ BAINNE BLÁTHACH

It's not the same thing. Literally, buttermilk isn't milk.

⟶ BAIN TRIAIL AS ⟵

Is maith liom bainne gabhair. I like goat's milk.

4. DORAS FEASA FIAFRAÍ

Enquiry is the door to knowledge. Ignore those who say, 'Curiosity killed the cat.' Curiosity is a good thing. It's how we learn. The American writer Studs Terkel left instructions that 'Curiosity didn't kill this cat' be inscribed on his headstone.

⟶ BAIN TRIAIL AS ⟵

Tá a fhios agam. I know.

5. AN TÉ A BHÍONN THUAS ÓLTAR DEOCH AIR AN TÉ A BHÍONN THÍOS BUAILTEAR COS AIR

When you're at the top you're a hero but when you're at the bottom you are zero (friendless). Literally, when you're up they toast you but when you're down they trample on you. The fickleness of human nature!

➳ BAIN TRIAIL AS ᏪᏆ

Luigh sé cos orm. He put his foot down.

6. BÍONN DHÁ INSINT AR SCÉAL

There are two sides to every story. An extension of this *seanfhocal* continues *agus dhá leagan déag ar amhrán* (and twelve versions of a song). Not surprising when we consider that storytelling and singing were our ancestors' principal entertainments *cois tine* (by the fire).

Seo é mo leagan den scéal.
This is my version of the story.

7. IS FADA AN BÓTHAR NACH mBÍONN CASADH ANN

It's a long road that has no turning. Nothing is ever straightforward. There's a twist in every story.

~@ BAIN TRIAIL AS @~

Bhí sé imithe ar chasadh do láimhe. He was gone in a moment (in the twist of your hand).

8. IS FEARR FUÍOLL AN MHADRA NÁ FUÍOLL AN MHAGAIDH

Better a dog's bite than a joker's jibe. *Fuíoll* literally means 'the leavings' or a bad outcome. So while a dog's bite may heal, a bitter word may do lasting damage.

Ní magadh ar bith é. It's no joke.

9. NÍ RAIBH CEANNACH NA MIONN AIR

He wasn't stuck for swear words. Literally, he didn't have to buy (*ceannach*) swear words (*mionn*) – he had plenty of his own! Obviously said of someone who had a 'loose tongue'!

Ceannach maith a bhí ann. It was a bargain.

10. IS AIT AN MAC AN SAOL

It's a funny old world. You never know what life can throw at you.

Is ait an duine é. He's an odd fellow.

11. BEAGÁN ACH É A DHÉANAMH GO MAITH

Do what you do do well. Literally, do only a little (*beagán*) but do it well. Do the basics well and a good performance will follow.

BAIN TRIAIL AS

Bíonn blas ar an mbeagán.
A little is tasty (or appreciated).

12. CHOMH CASTA LE hADHARCA GABHAIR

As twisted as the horns of a goat. Said of a story or an account that is almost too intricate to follow.

BAIN TRIAIL AS

Tá gruaig chasta aici. She has curly hair.

13. AR DHEIS DÉ GO RAIBH A (h-) ANAM

May he/she rest in peace. Literally, may his/her soul be at God's right hand. A blessing for the deceased. Other blessings are: *Suaimhneas síoraí dó/ di* (Eternal peace to him/her); *Solas na bhFlaitheas dó/di* (Light of heaven to him/her).

➶ BAIN TRIAIL AS ❧

Ar mo lámh dheas/ar mo lámh chlé.
On my right hand/on my left hand.

14. IS MAIRG A BHÍONN GAN DEARTHÁIR

Woe to him who is without a brother – not necessarily a blood brother but a supporter in time of need. A variant on *Ní neart go cur le chéile* (United we stand).

➶ BAIN TRIAIL AS ❧

Tá beirt dearthái agam. I have two brothers.

15. NA TRÍ GLÓRTHA IS BINNE – MEILT BHRÓ, GÉIMNEACH BÓ IS BÉIC LINBH

The three sweetest sounds – a milling quernstone, the lowing of a cow and the cry of a child. Another 'three'. Not many quernstones around nowadays, so what would be our three sweetest sounds? *Crónán na mbeach* (humming of bees)? *Ceol an loin dhuibh* (the singing of the blackbird)? *Glór uisce* (the sound of water)?

◦ BAIN TRIAIL AS *◦*

An glór is binne dár chuala mé riamh.
The sweetest voice I ever heard.

16. IS FEARR SUÍ INA AICE NÁ SUÍ INA ÁIT

Better sit beside him than in his place. Sometimes the 'hot seat' or being in charge is not the best place to be.

Tá cónaí orm in aice an bhaile. I live near the town.

17. NÁ hÉILIGH DO CHEART GO bhFEICFEAR DO NEART

Don't demand your rights (*do cheart*) until you know your strength (*do neart*). Weigh your options carefully. Sometimes discretion is the better part of valour.

❧ BAIN TRIAIL AS ☙

Ní ceart é sin a dhéanamh. It's not right to do that.

18. TURAS IN AISCE A BHÍ ANN

It was a wasted journey. A useless venture.

❧ BAIN TRIAIL AS ☙

Saor in aisce. Free, gratis, no charge.

19. IS MÓ A THAIBHSE NÁ A THAIRBHE

It looks better than it is. Literally, its appearance (*taibhse*) is greater than its use (*tairbhe*). Don't be fooled by appearances.

Bhain mé tairbhe as an turas sin.
I benefitted from that journey.

20. TÁ A PHORT SEINNTE

He's finished with, undone. Literally, his tune (*port*) is played (*seinnte*). *Tá deireadh leis. Tá a ré thart.* His time is up.

Seinn port dúinn! Play us a tune!

21. TUAR AN t-ÁDH AGUS TIOCFAIDH SÉ

Expect good luck and it will come. Always look on the bright side. Yes we can!

☙ BAIN TRIAIL AS ❧

Bhí an t-ádh leat. You were lucky.

22. IS MÓ CRAICEANN A CHUIREANN AN ÓIGE DI

Youth sheds many a skin (*craiceann*). The young person goes through many phases in the process of growing up.

☙ BAIN TRIAIL AS ❧

Bhí mé fliuch go craiceann. I was wet to the skin.

23. NÍ BHAILÍONN CLOCH REATHA CAONACH

A rolling stone gathers no moss. Well, look at Mick Jagger – rolling for over half a century and not a sign of moss! Keep yourself busy and all will be well.

❧ BAIN TRIAIL AS ❧

Cúrsaí reatha. Current affairs.

24. NÍOR GHABH TAOIDE SIAR NÁ GO nGABHFAIDH TAOIDE ANIAR

No tide ever went out without returning. Life goes on while everything passes. Another variation: *Níl tuile dá mhéid nach dtránn* (Even the largest tide ebbs).

❧ BAIN TRIAIL AS ❧

Gabh mo leithscéal. Excuse me/Accept my apology.

25. NÍL LUIBH NÁ LEIGHEAS IN AGHAIDH AN BHÁIS

There's no avoiding death. Literally, there isn't a herb (*luibh*) or a cure (*leigheas*) in the face of death. Along with taxes, death is a great certainty. *Nuair a thiocfaidh an bás ní imeoidh sé folamh* (When death comes, it won't leave empty).

⤳ BAIN TRIAIL AS ⤶

Níl leigheas agam air. I cannot help it.

26. CUAIRT GHEARR IS Í IS FEARR

A short visit (*cuairt*) is best. Don't overstay your welcome.

⤳ BAIN TRIAIL AS ⤶

Tabhair cuairt orainn. Pay us a visit.

27. BEATHA TEANGA Í A LABHAIRT

A language lives by being spoken. Even if you only have *beagán Gaeilge* (a little Irish), *labhair í* (speak it). Keep it alive.

⟨∘⟩ BAIN TRIAIL AS ⟨∘⟩

Labhair Gaeilge más féidir leat.
Speak Irish if you can.

28. NÍL ANN ACH AN DÁ MAR A CHÉILE

They are both the same. Six of one, a half dozen of the other.

⟨∘⟩ BAIN TRIAIL AS ⟨∘⟩

D'imigh said i ndiaidh a chéile.
They went one after another.

29. NÍ DHÍOLANN DEARMAD FIACHA

Forgetting does not pay off debts. If you have debts (*fiacha*) forgetting about them is no excuse. Pay them off.

BAIN TRIAIL AS

Rinne mé dearmad air. I forgot it.

30. IS GEALL AR AN gCAT A CHRAICEANN

You can't have one without the other. Literally, the cat goes with his skin. If you have one, you have the other. *Geall* is a pledge or a bet.

BAIN TRIAIL AS

Cuirim geall leat. I bet you.

31. TÓGFAIDH DATH DUBH ACH NÍ THÓGFAIDH DUBH DATH

It's easier to ruin someone's reputation than to restore it. Literally, colour (*dath*) will take black but black won't take colour. Be careful what you say about someone.

❧ BAIN TRIAIL AS ❧

D'imigh sé gan dubh gan dath.
He left without a trace.

Focailín

You will surprise yourself at how much you can build your Irish vocabulary around a *Focailín* (little word) like:

Gach	Each or every
Gach duine	Everyone
Gach lá	Every day
Gach aon rud	Everything
Gach a bhfuil agam	Everything I have
Gach sort oibre	Every kind of work
Gach uair	Every time
Gach mac máthar	Every mother's son
Gach a chonaic mé	Everything I saw
Gach re duine	Every second (other) person
Gach re sea	Tit for tat

AUGUST
Lúnara

1. GO dTÉ TÚ SLÁN

May you go safely. A simple blessing for someone departing on a journey. Similarly, *Go n-éirí do thuras leat* (May your journey be successful).

⟿ BAIN TRIAIL AS ⟿

Slán abhaile. Safe home.

2. NÍ FIÚ SEILE NA CUAICHE É

He's not worth a 'cuckoo spit'. He's totally worthless. A fairly damning summation of an opponent.

⟿ BAIN TRIAIL AS ⟿

Is fiú é a dhéanamh. It's worth doing.

3. IS MINIC A BHÍ CÚ MHALL SONA

Often the slow dog is lucky. The race can throw up misfortune for the fastest dog – a stumble, an argument with another dog. Similarly, for the race of life.

BAIN TRIAIL AS

Nollaig shona duit. Happy Christmas to you.

4. NUAIR A THIOCFAIDH AMÁRACH, TIOCFAIDH A CHUID

Tomorrow will provide for itself. Literally, when tomorrow comes, its portion/share will come. Don't worry about tomorrow; look after today.

BAIN TRIAIL AS

Fuair tú an chuid is fearr. You got the best part.

5. NÍOR DHÚN DIA DORAS RIAMH NÁR OSCAIL SÉ CEANN EILE

God never closed one door without opening another. A much-quoted tribute to Divine Providence. Everything will be fine.

BAIN TRIAIL AS

Tabhair an doras dó! Show him the door!

6. TRÍ RUD NACH FÉIDIR A FHEICEÁIL – FAOBHAR, GAOTH AGUS GRÁ

Three things you can't see – an 'edge', the wind and love. Another 'three'.

BAIN TRIAIL AS

Faobhar lae is oíche. Twilight.
Literally, the edge of day and night.

7. CHUIRFEADH SÉ COSA FAOI CHEARCA DUIT

He's a very handy individual. Literally, he would put legs on hens. A clever fellow, indeed.

⤙ BAIN TRIAIL AS ⤚

Chuaigh mé ann de chois. I went there on foot.

8. BÍONN AN FHÍRINNE SEARBH

The truth is bitter. However much it hurts, the truth must be faced.

⤙ BAIN TRIAIL AS ⤚

Tá blas searbh ar an deoch sin.
There's a bitter taste to that drink.

9. NÍ SHEASANN SAC FOLAMH

An empty sack won't stand. Food sustains us all. Another variation: *Ní fhéadfadh mála folamh seasamh, ná cat marbh siúl* (An empty sack won't stand, nor will a dead cat walk).

⟶ BAIN TRIAIL AS ⟵

Bhí an teach folamh. The house was empty.

10. IDIR AN LAG IS AN LOM

In the balance. Literally, (in reference to the tide) between the ebb and the flow.

⟶ BAIN TRIAIL AS ⟵

Tá an mála lomlán. The sack is full to the brim.

11. MOLANN AN OBAIR AN FEAR

The work proclaims the man. I am reminded of the Latin inscription in St Paul's Cathedral in London regarding its architect, Sir Christopher Wren, *Si monumentum requiris, circumspice* (If you seek his monument, look around you).

⮾ BAIN TRIAIL AS ⮾

Moladh le Dia. God be praised.

12. CEILEANN AN GRÁ AINIMH IS LOCHT

Love is blind! Love can hide defects and faults. Let's be careful out there.

⮾ BAIN TRIAIL AS ⮾

Níl sé gan locht. He's not without fault.

13. RITHEANN UISCE DOIMHIN CIÚIN

Still waters run deep. I may be silent but it doesn't mean I'm not thinking. As another *seanfhocal* says, *Is iad na muca ciúine a itheas an mhin* (It's the quiet pigs that eat the meal).

⟋⟍ BAIN TRIAIL AS ⟍⟋

An Fear Ciúin – cad é mar scannán!
The Quiet Man – what a film!

14. AN DUINE FÉIN IS FEARR A FHIOS CÁ LUÍONN AN BHRÓG AIR

The wearer knows best how the shoe fits him. Consult those directly involved.

⟋⟍ BAIN TRIAIL AS ⟍⟋

Cá bhfios duit? How do you know?

15. NÍ MÚINEADH GO DEA-SHAMPLA

Good example is the best teacher. Do as I do, not
as I say.

Ní mhúinfeadh an saol é. Nothing could teach him.

16. NÍL ANN ACH SCRÍOBADH
AN CHRÚISCÍN

It's only the 'scrapings of the jar', usually referring
to the 'runt' or young of a litter. Something weak
or helpless.

Tá mé ag scríobadh dom féin.
I'm looking after myself.

17. IS DÓIGH LE FEAR NA BUILE GURB É FÉIN FEAR NA CÉILLE

The crazy one thinks that he is the most sensible. When rage takes over, sense (*ciall*) goes out the window. Calm down before you act.

BAIN TRIAIL AS

Bhí mé ar buile. I was raging.

18. AN CHEARC AR FAD IS AN t-ANRAITH

The full story. Literally, the whole hen (*chearc*) and the soup (*anraith*). The entire menu is on offer.

BAIN TRIAIL AS

Anraith te, lá fuar. Sin deas!
Hot soup on a cold day. That's nice!

19. LIG LIOMSA IS LIGFIDH MÉ LEATSA

Don't bother me and I won't bother you. To each his own.

⟶ BAIN TRIAIL AS ⟵

Lig isteach mé. Let me in.

20. NUAIR IS MÓ AN SPÓRT, IS CÓIR STAD DE

Quit when you are ahead. When enjoyment is at its highest, that's the time to stop.

⟶ BAIN TRIAIL AS ⟵

Níl ceart ná cóir aige. He is entirely in the wrong. Literally, he has neither right nor justice.

21. NÍ HÍ AN BHEAN IS ÁILLE IS TROIME CIALL

Beauty and brains don't always go hand in hand. Literally, the most beautiful woman isn't necessarily the one of greatest intellect.

⟿ BAIN TRIAIL AS ⟿

An áit is áille sa tír.
The loveliest place in the country.

22. NÍL MAITH SA SEANCHAS NUAIR A BHÍOS AN ANACHAIN DÉANTA

There's no good in talking when the damage is done. Or even crying over spilt milk. Move on with your life.

⟿ BAIN TRIAIL AS ⟿

Tá siad ag seanchas le chéile. They are gossiping.

23. DHÉANFADH DEALG SPÍONÁIN BRAON LEIS

Even a gooseberry thorn can cause a sore. Great evils can sometimes have a small cause. Dinneen's dictionary tells us that Virginia, Co. Cavan, was known as *Beirdsinigh bheag na spíonán* (little Virginia of the gooseberries) because a gooseberry fair was once held there.

⟿ BAIN TRIAIL AS ⟿

Chuaigh dealg i mo mhéar.
A thorn went into my finger.

24. GACH CAT DE RÉIR CINEÁIL

Every cat according to its kind. A variation of *Briseann an dúchas trí shúile an chait* (Nature/ instinct breaks through the eyes of a cat). A cat will do what a cat will do. This also applies to many two-legged 'cats'.

Ta cineál an cheoil ann. He is musical by nature.

25.   NÍL AON DLÍ AR AN RIACHTANAS

Necessity knows no law. When need is greatest it is not amenable to law. A great motion for a debate?

Tá sé riachtanach. It is necessary/compulsory.

26.   IS OLC AN GHAOTH NACH SÉIDEANN DO DHUINE ÉIGIN

It's an ill wind that blows no good for somebody. No matter how awful the circumstances or the event, somebody will benefit.

Fuair mé gaoth an fhocail.
I got a hint. Literally, I got wind of the word.

27. IS GIORRA DO DHUINE A CHRAICEANN NÁ A LÉINE

Your own problems come first. Literally, a person's skin is nearer than his shirt.

⌐⊸ BAIN TRIAIL AS ⊶⌐

Is gearr go dtiocfaidh sé. He will arrive soon.

28. NÁ hALTAIGH DO BHIA GO mBEIDH SÉ I DO MHÁLA

Don't count your chickens. Literally, don't acknowledge your food until it's in your bag. Wait until everything is signed, sealed and delivered before you say thanks.

⌐⊸ BAIN TRIAIL AS ⊶⌐

Altú roimh bhia/tar éis bia.
Grace before/after meals.

29. RINNE SÉ OBAIR NA gCAPALL

He did the heavy work. Literally, the work of horses. A phrase popular with sports commentators, describing the role of the player who does the unglamorous tackling and carrying work, as opposed to the 'stars' who make the headlines.

◦◦◦ BAIN TRIAIL AS ◦◦◦

Obair éadrom. Light work.

30. D'IMIGH GACH RUD TÓIN THAR CEANN ORM

Everything went topsy-turvy on me. It all fell apart. Alternatively, *bun os cionn* (head over heels/ upside down).

◦◦◦ BAIN TRIAIL AS ◦◦◦

Thug mé tóin leis. I turned my back on him.

31. SAOL FADA CHUGAINN AGUS BÁS IN ÉIRINN

Long life to us – and death in Ireland. A toast to which we all drink.

⟿ BAIN TRIAIL AS ⟾

Tá a fhios ag an saol. The whole world knows.

Focailín

You will surprise yourself at how much you can build your Irish vocabulary around a *Focailín* (little word) like:

Thar	Across/over/beyond
Thar barr	Excellent
Thar sáile	Overseas
Thar ceann	In place of
Thar mo chumas	Beyond my ability
Thar mo dhóthain	Too much for me
Thar am	Beyond the time
Thar gach ní	Above everything
Thar fóir	Beyond help
Thar fulaingt	Beyond endurance
Thar m'eolas	Beyond my ken

SEPTEMBER

meán fómhaiṟ

1. TIGH I mBÉAL BÓTHAIR, NÍ AISTEAR É ACH CÓNGAR

A friendly house shortens the road. In the days when a *céilí* or friendly call into a house was more common, such a visit was not a journey (*aistear*) but a shortcut (*cóngar*) offering respite and welcome. Happier days!

∽ BAIN TRIAIL AS ∼

Ní aistear dom dul ann.
It's no trouble for me to go there.

2.   CRUTHÚ NA PUTÓIGE A hITHE

The proof of the pudding is in the eating. The actual experience of something (rather than talking about it) will prove its worth.

Is maith liom putóg Nollag.
I like Christmas pudding.

3.   CUIR LUATH AGUS BAIN LUATH

Sow early and reap early. Farming advice that can be applied to life in general. The sooner you invest your time/effort, the sooner you will reap the benefit.

Chomh luath is a chuala mé an scéal, tháinig mé.
I came as soon as I heard the news.

4. IS PRÁINNEACH AN FEAR AN FÓMHAR

Autumn (harvest-time) is a busy fellow, especially on the farm where there is much to be done before winter comes.

꧁ BAIN TRIAIL AS ꧂

PRÁINNEACH! Léigh é seo, le do thoil.
URGENT! Please read this.

5. IS MILIS DÁ ÓL É ACH IS SEARBH DÁ ÍOC É

It's sweet to drink, but bitter to pay for. Referring to alcohol, of course. Bitter (*searbh*) to pay for, not just in terms of money, but in the misery and damage it can bring. A salutary warning. *Is é an brón deireadh na meisce* (Sorrow is the end of drunkenness).

꧁ BAIN TRIAIL AS ꧂

Dhíol mé go dona as. I paid badly for it.

6. I gCOSA DUINE A BHÍOS A SHLÁINTE

A person's health is in his feet. Referring to a time when people travelled by foot. My mother always said, 'Never skimp on a pair of shoes. Your feet are your health.' A wise woman.

BAIN TRIAIL AS

Thug sé na cosa leis. He escaped.

7. AN GHAOTH ADUAIDH, BÍONN SÍ CRUA AN GHAOTH ANEAS, BÍONN SÍ TAIS AN GHAOTH ANOIR, BÍONN SÍ TIRIM AN GHAOTH ANIAR, BÍONN SÍ FIAL

Harsh is the north wind
But the south wind blows fresh
A dry wind from the east
But the west wind is kind

A little rhyme about the four winds.

Saol crua a bhí ann. They were hard times.

8.   PÍOBAIRE AN AON PHOIRT

A one-tuned piper. Johnny one-note. Someone whose horizons are limited and who goes on and on with the one story.

Is binn an port é. It's a sweet tune.

9.   IS CRUA CORAÍ AN tSAOIL

Life is full of ups and downs. Literally, life's twists (*coraí*) are hard.

Féach an cor atá air. Look at the state of him.

10.   NÍ RAIBH GÍOG NÁ MÍOG AS

There wasn't a squeak out of him. He was very quiet indeed.

⟿ BAIN TRIAIL AS ⟿

Ní raibh míog codlata agam.
I hadn't a wink of sleep.

11.   MURACH M'ATHAIR,
   DHÉANFAINN CATHAIR

If it weren't for my father I'd have built a city. There's always someone else to blame for one's shortcomings. I could have been a contender!

⟿ BAIN TRIAIL AS ⟿

Murach mise, bheadh deireadh leat.
If it weren't for me, you were finished.

12. FÉASTA ANOCHT AGUS GORTA AMÁRACH

A feast tonight, a famine tomorrow. There are good times and lean times. So it goes with some people. *Thuas seal agus thíos seal.*

⟿ BAIN TRIAIL AS ⟾

An Gorta Mór. The Great Famine.

13. DÁ MBEADH A FHIOS AGAM BHEADH LEIGHEAS AGAM

If I had the knowledge I'd have the cure. Sometimes it's best to acknowledge that we have limitations. There are some things that are beyond our ken.

⟿ BAIN TRIAIL AS ⟾

An bhfuil a fhios agat faoi sin?
Do you know about that?

14. NÍOR THÁINIG TRIOBLÓID RIAMH INA hAONAR

Trouble never came alone. Some would say troubles come in threes, but a trouble on its own certainly doesn't mean the end of misfortune.

BAIN TRIAIL AS

Tá sí ansin ina haonar. She's there on her own.

15. IS RAIMHRE FUIL NÁ UISCE

Blood is thicker than water. A blood relationship will always win out before any other.

BAIN TRIAIL AS

Tá mé ag cur fola. I am bleeding.

16.   NÍ LÚ MO MHAOIN NÁ MO MHUIRÍN

I make ends meet. Literally, my wealth is no less than my family. I get by.

BAIN TRIAIL AS

Tá muirín mhór aige. He has a large family.

17.   IS MINIC A MHAOLAIGH BÉILE MAITH BRÓN

A good meal often eases sorrow.

BAIN TRIAIL AS

Tá brón orm faoi sin. I'm sorry about that.

18. GACH AON DUINE IS A GHALAR FÉIN AIR

Everyone has their own troubles. Literally, everyone has his own disease (*galar*). Nobody is immune from some affliction.

⟡ BAIN TRIAIL AS ⟡

Galar gan leigheas. An incurable disease.

19. TAITHÍ A DHÉANANN MÁISTREACHT

Practice makes perfect. Literally, experience makes mastery.

⟡ BAIN TRIAIL AS ⟡

Níl aon teorainn le taithí.
There is no limit to experience.

20. BEAN MHIC IS MÁTHAIR CHÉILE MAR A BHEADH CAT IS LUCH AR AGHAIDH A CHÉILE

The daughter-in-law and the mother-in-law – like a cat and a mouse facing each other. There is no more to be said!

⤚❧ BAIN TRIAIL AS ❧⤙

Bean an tí. The woman of the house.

21. NÍ FHAIGHTEAR SAILL GAN SAOTHRÚ

No sweat (*saill*) without hard work. Nothing comes easy. You've got to work hard for success.

⤚❧ BAIN TRIAIL AS ❧⤙

Tá sé ag saothrú an léinn.
He is cultivating learning.

22. CHUIR SÉ FÁILTE IS FICHE ROMHAM

He gave me a great welcome. Literally, he gave me twenty-one welcomes.

_____ BAIN TRIAIL AS _____

Fiche bliain ag fás. Twenty years a-growing.

23. NÁ BÍ LUATH CHUN LABHARTHA NÁ LEASC CHUN ÉISTEACHTA

Don't be quick to speak or slow to listen. Fools rush in where angels fear to tread, so be measured in your response to a situation.

_____ BAIN TRIAIL AS _____

Tá mé ag labhairt leat agus níl tú ag éisteacht. I'm speaking to you and you're not listening.

24. IS CUMA NÓ MUC DUINE GAN SEIFT

A person without a plan is no better than a pig. Here we go again – dismissing the poor pig. Shameless! The essence of the *seanfhocal* is – be prepared. But go easy on the pig.

~ BAIN TRIAIL AS ~

Is cuma liom. I don't care.

25. MURA nDÉANA SÉ LÁ PRÁTAÍ A BHAINT DÉANFAIDH SÉ LÁ CÁRTAÍ A IMIRT

If it's not a day for picking potatoes it will be a day for playing cards. There's always an alternative, maybe even a more pleasurable one. An admirable philosophy of life!

~ BAIN TRIAIL AS ~

Is breá liom a bheith ag imirt cártaí.
I love playing cards.

26. IS MÓ A SCIOBÓL NÁ A IOTHLAINN

His barn (*scioból*) is bigger than his haggard (*iothlainn*). He expects more than he is likely to get. He has high ambitions.

ᴮᴬᴵᴺ BAIN TRIAL AS

In iothlainn Dé go gcastar sinn. May we meet up in God's haggard. A line from the old Irish poem and song 'Ag Críost an Síol'.

27. TÁ SÉ IMITHE AR SHLÍ NA FÍRINNE

He is dead. Literally, he is gone on the righteous way, the way of truth.

BAIN TRIAL AS

Mo shlí bheatha. My livelihood.

28. AN BÉAL BOCHT

The poor mouth. Used to describe someone who is endlessly complaining. *Ní fhaca mé riamh é ach an béal bocht aige* (I never saw him but he was grumbling about something). Myles na gCopaleen wrote a satirical novel with this title.

⤙ BAIN TRIAIL AS ⤚

Ó bhéal go béal. By word of mouth.

29. TÁILLIÚIR, PÍOBAIRE AGUS GABHAR – AN TRIÚR IS AERAÍ AR DOMHAN

A tailor, a piper and a goat – the three liveliest (giddiest) creatures on earth. Another 'three'. I'm not sure how the tailor got into such company.

⤙ BAIN TRIAIL AS ⤚

Tá triúr mac aici. She has three sons.

30. IS SEARBH GACH GNÁTH

One gets tired of the same old thing. Literally, the commonplace becomes bitter.

Is gnáth leis dul ag siúl. He usually goes walking.

Focailín

You will surprise yourself at how much you can build your Irish vocabulary around a *Focailín* (little word) like:

De	Out of/from
De ghnáth	As a rule
De bharr	As a result of
De ló is d'oíche	By day and night
De chois	By foot
De bhrí	By reason of
De shíor	Forever
De ghlanmheabhair	By rote
De thraein	By rail
D'aon ghuth	With one voice
De mo thoil féin	Of my own will

OCTOBER

᛫Deᚋᛖᚪᛞᚻ
ᚠóᛘᚺᚪᛁᛁ

1. IS FEARR FÉACHAINT ROMHAT NÁ DHÁ FHÉACHAINT I DO DHIAIDH

One look ahead is better than two looks behind. What's done is done. Leave the past behind and look to the future.

⟡ BAIN TRIAIL AS ⟡

Féach romhat! Look out!

2. BÍONN BLAS MILIS AR PHRAISEACH NA gCOMHARSAN

The neighbour's porridge has a sweet taste. Do you remember when what you wouldn't eat at home always tasted better in someone else's house?

A variation on, 'The other man's grass is always greener.'

Rinne mé praiseach de.
I made a mess of it.

3. AN TAOBH SLEAMHAIN AMUIGH AGUS AN TAOBH CAM ISTIGH

The slippery side out and the twisted side within. A rogue of the first degree. To be avoided at all costs!

⁓ BAIN TRIAL AS ⁓

Tá an bóthar sleamhain go leor.
The road is slippery enough.

4.   TÁ MÉ AR MHUIN NA MUICE

I'm on the pig's back. Life is good. 'Made it, Ma! Top of the world!'

BAIN TRIAIL AS

Tháinig sé ar muin capaill. He came on horseback.

5.   FICHE BLIAIN AG TEACHT
FICHE BLIAIN GO MAITH
FICHE BLIAIN AG MEATH
FICHE BLIAIN GAN RATH

Twenty years up and coming
Twenty years on top
Twenty years in decline
Twenty years without blessing

In a word – LIFE! (in one person's view)

BAIN TRIAIL AS

Tá sí fiche bliain d'aois. She is twenty years old.

6. NÍ MEASA LIOM SIOC SAN FHÓMHAR NÁ É

I'd prefer anything to that. Literally, it's worse than an autumn frost. It's the worst thing possible.

⟿ BAIN TRIAIL AS ⟾

Tá sé ag cur seaca amuigh. It's freezing outside.

7. TÚS AGUS DEIREADH AN DUINE TARRAINGT AR AN TINE

At the beginning and the end of life we are drawn to the fire. The child is fascinated by the magic of the flames. The old person seeks warmth and comfort – and maybe a song or a story. The hearth is central to all our lives.

⟿ BAIN TRIAIL AS ⟾

Sin tús agus deireadh an scéil.
That's the beginning and the end of the story.

8. AN CÓNGAR CHUN AN BHIA IS AN TIMPEALL CHUN NA hOIBRE

The shortcut to food and the long road to work. The promise of food is often preferable to the prospect of work. The spirit may be willing, but the flesh is invariably weak.

⤙⤙ BAIN TRIAIL AS ⤚⤚

Cas anseo agus glac an cóngar.
Turn here and take the shortcut.

9. NÍL AON BHANNA NÁ TAGANN A DHÁTA

Everything runs its course. Literally, there is no bond/promise that hasn't got its (redemption) date. Every account will eventually be settled.

⤙⤙ BAIN TRIAIL AS ⤚⤚

Sin mo dháta breithe. That's my date of birth.

10. IS MAITH AN CUAN AN CÚINNE

The nook is a safe harbour. The nook (*cúinne*) here is the corner seat by the fire, a place of warmth and security, a safe harbour (*cuan*).

◦⟋ BAIN TRIAIL AS ⟍◦

Suigh ansin sa chúinne. Sit there in the corner.

11. IS DEACAIR CEANN CRÍONNA A CHUR AR CHOLAINN ÓG

It's hard to put a wise head on young shoulders. A variation of *Tagann ciall le haois* (Sense comes with age).

◦⟋ BAIN TRIAIL AS ⟍◦

Is deacair é a thuiscint. It's hard to understand.

12. CUIR AN BREAC SAN EANGACH SULA gCUIRE TÚ SA PHOTA É

Don't count your chickens. Literally, before you put the trout in the pot you must put him in the net (*eangach*). A variation of *Ní breac go bruach é* (It's not a trout [until it's landed]). Or as Mrs Beeton said regarding hare soup, 'First, catch your hare.'

⌘ BAIN TRIAIL AS ⌘

Tá an liathróid báite san eangach aige. He has buried the ball in the net. He has scored a goal.

13. NÍL ANN ACH SCEACH I mBÉAL BEARNA

It's only a stopgap. Literally, it's only a bush (*sceach*) in the gap (*bearna*).

⌘ BAIN TRIAIL AS ⌘

Seachain an bhearna! Mind the gap!

14. IS FEARR AN t-IMREAS NÁ AN t-UAIGNEAS

Competition is better than loneliness. Better to have someone to challenge you than to sit there on your own – and wither. Competition is the life of trade.

⤙ BAIN TRIAIL AS ⤚

Is deacair an rud an t-uaigneas.
Loneliness is a 'hard oul' station'.

15. IS MAIRG A FHAIGHEANN SÓLÁS I nDÓLÁS A CHOMHARSAN

Woe (*mairg*) to him who delights in his neighbour's misfortunes. Rejoice in your neighbour's success and support him in his tribulations. Never strike a man when he is down.

⤙ BAIN TRIAIL AS ⤚

Is beag sólás a fuair mé. I got little comfort.

16. IS LEOR DON DREOILÍN A NEAD

The wren's nest is all she needs. For some, contentment is easily found. For the wren, it's the comfort of her home.

BAIN TRIAIL AS

Ar thóir an dreoilín Lá 'le Stiofáin.
Hunting the wren on St Stephen's Day.

17. NÍOR CHUIR SÉ AON FHIACAL ANN

He didn't mince his words. Literally, he didn't put a tooth in it. He told it exactly as he saw it.

BAIN TRIAIL AS

Tá tinneas fiacaile orm. I have a toothache.

18. TÁ SIAD FITE FUAITE TRÍD A CHÉILE

They are totally intermingled. Literally, they are woven (*fite*) and sewn (*fuaite*) into each other. A total tangle!

BAIN TRIAIL AS

Is fuath liom fuáil. I hate sewing.

19. BUILLE MARFA NA MUICE

The killer blow. Literally, the blow that finally killed the pig. A phrase beloved by sports commentators to describe a score that decided the outcome of a game.

BAIN TRIAIL AS

Buille faoi thuairim. A mere guess.

20. BHÍ SÉ I nGREIM AN DÁ BHRUACH

He stayed on the fence, uncommitted. Literally, he
had a grip (*greim*) on both banks (of a river).

BAIN TRIAIL AS

Greim an duine bháite.
The drowning man's grip. A desperate hold.

21. BREATHNAIGH/FÉACH
AN ABHAINN SULA dTÉIR
INA CUILITHE

Look before you leap. Literally, examine the river
(*abha*) before you enter its current (*cuilithe*). Test
the waters before you embark on a venture.

BAIN TRIAIL AS

Tá tú ag breathnú go maith. You are looking well.

22. IS GEALL LE SOS MALAIRT OIBRE

A change of work (*malairt oibre*) is as good as a rest (*sos*). Try something different.

~ BAIN TRIAIL AS ~

Tóg sos ar feadh tamaill. Take a break for a while.

23. TÁ EIREABALL AN CHAIT SA GHRÍOSACH

There's bad weather on the way. How do we know? Because the cat's tail (*eireaball an chait*) is in the embers (*gríosach*), practically in the fire. Watch the cat. He knows stuff!

~ BAIN TRIAIL AS ~

Is é gnó an chait luch a mharú.
It's the cat's business to kill a mouse.

24. AN RÓGAIRE IS CAIME, DÉANANN AN BÁS FEAR DÍREACH DE

Death is the great leveller. Literally, death (*bás*) will straighten out the most twisted rogue. There is no escape!

༷ BAIN TRIAIL AS ༷

An módh díreach. The direct method.

25. NÁ TRÉIG CARA AR DO CHUID

Don't abandon (*tréig*) a friend for your own selfish reasons. True friendship is precious. Cherish it rather than abandon it.

༷ BAIN TRIAIL AS ༷

Is tú mo chara dhílis. You are my faithful friend.

26. IS DALL SÚIL I gCÚIL DUINE EILE

You never know what goes on behind closed doors.
Literally, an eye is blind (*dall*) in another person's
corner (*cúil*). A stranger in a house doesn't know
what goes on there.

◦＞ BAIN TRIAIL AS ◦＜

Dubh agus dall na hoíche.
The darkness and gloom of night.

27. DÍOL SAOR IS CEANNAIGH
DAOR IS BEIDH DO BHOTÚN ORT

Sell cheap and buy dear and you'll pay for it.
Literally, sell cheap and buy dear and the mistake
(*botún*) is yours. Fairly basic business advice. The
opposite – *Díol daor is ceannaigh saor* (Sell dear and
buy cheap) – should be the goal.

◦＞ BAIN TRIAIL AS ◦＜

Rinne mé botún. I made a mistake.

28. NÍOR AONTAIGH MÉ LEIS – DUBH, BÁN NÁ RIABHACH

I didn't agree with that at all – at all. Literally, I didn't agree – black, white or striped. Total non-acceptance.

Bó riabhach. A brindled cow.

29. CUIRIM RUD AR AN MÉAR FHADA

I put something on the long finger. I procrastinate. Another *seanfhocal* says: *Is éasca nóin ná maidin* (Things are easier done in the evening).

Mo mhéara coise. My toes.

30. CHOMH hÉADROM LE CAT I gCLÓS COMHARSAN

As light-footed as a cat in a neighbour's yard. The cat knows he shouldn't be there, so he is particularly wary.

BAIN TRIAIL AS

Tá na páistí amuigh sa chlós.
The children are out in the yard.

31. CEANN CÍORTHA A DHÍOLAS NA COSA

Clothes make the man. Literally, the combed head sells the feet. Good grooming will hide a lot of defects.

BAIN TRIAIL AS

Stampaí ar díol anseo. Stamps sold here.

Focailín

You will surprise yourself at how much you can build your Irish vocabulary around a *Focailín* (little word) like:

As	Out of
As seo	Out of here
As baile	Away from home
As obair	Out of work
As gach treo	From every direction
As anáil	Out of breath
As radharc	Out of view
As sin amach	From then on
As a chéile	Asunder
As a mheabhair	Out of his mind
As láthair	Absent

NOVEMBER
Samhain

1. TÁ MÍ NA MARBH LINN

The month of the dead is here. In both pagan and Christian times, November is associated with remembering those who have died, as well as with the end of the harvest season (*fómhar*) and the onset of winter.

 BAIN TRIAIL AS

Beannacht Dé leis na mairbh.
God bless the departed.

2. IS MAITH AN NÍ AN ÓIGE ACH NÍ THAGANN SÍ FAOI DHÓ

Youth is wonderful, but it doesn't come twice. So, make the most of it. Don't let it be said that 'youth is wasted on the young'.

➠ **BAIN TRIAIL AS** ⬳

Bhuaigh siad an corn faoi dhó.
They won the cup twice.

3. TÓG AN FÁL NÓ ÍOCFAIDH TÚ AN FOGHAIL

Prevention is better than cure. Literally, mend the fence (*fál*) or you'll pay for the plunder (*foghail*). The 'fence' may be literal or metaphorical.

➠ **BAIN TRIAIL AS** ⬳

Íocfaidh tú as sin lá éigin.
Someday you'll pay for that.

4. NÍ FEARR DUIT CÁITH
I DO MHÁLA NÁ MIN

You don't know a good thing when you have it. Literally, having chaff (*cáith*) in your bag is worse than having it full of meal (*min*). Appreciate the good things you have.

 BAIN TRIAIL AS

An rud is fearr a rinne mé riamh.
The best thing I ever did.

5. IS MÓR AN SÓLÁS
AN GHLAINEACHT

Cleanliness (*glaineacht*) is a great comfort. Or as the English proverb says, 'Cleanliness is next to Godliness.'

 BAIN TRIAIL AS

Tá mé glan de. I am free of him.

6.   TÚS NA hEAGNA UAMHAN DÉ

The fear (*uamhan*) of God is the beginning of wisdom (*eagna*). A translation from the Book of Proverbs (1:7).

BAIN TRIAIL AS

Cuir tús leis an obair. Make a start on the work.

7.   BÍONN NIMH AR AN AITHNE

Forbidden fruit is tempting. Literally, recognition (*aithne*) brings poison (*nimh*). Remember what happened over that apple in the Garden of Eden!

BAIN TRIAIL AS

Aire! Nimh! Caution! Poison!

8. IS MINIC A BHÍONN BREÁ BRÉAN

The beautiful can often be corrupt. Don't be fooled by appearances. A similar *seanfhocal* says, *Is fearr béasa ná breáthacht* (Manners are preferable to beauty).

⟿ BAIN TRIAIL AS ⟾

Tá mé bréan díot. I've had enough of you.

9. IS FEARR GORADH CÚL COS NÁ FICHE BÓ AR CHNOC

Toasting your legs by the fire is better than having twenty cows on the hill. Being a person of substance is no guarantee of contentment.

⟿ BAIN TRIAIL AS ⟾

Déan do ghoradh cois tine.
Warm yourself at the fire.

10. BHEARRFADH SÉ LUCH INA CHODLADH

He would shave a sleeping mouse. Said of a light-fingered person.

~∞ **BAIN TRIAIL AS** ∞~

Téigh a chodladh! Go asleep!

11. IS FEARR BOTHÁN LÁN NÁ CAISLEÁN FOLAMH

A cabin (*bothán*) that has plenty is better than an empty castle. Appearances can be deceptive. A humble little house that is full of warmth and love is better than a fine mansion that is cold and loveless.

~∞ **BAIN TRIAIL AS** ∞~

Póca folamh. An empty pocket.

12. COS IN UAIGH IS COS EILE AR AN mBRUACH

One foot in the grave and the other on the bank. A dire situation indeed. Little room for manoeuvre here.

BAIN TRIAIL AS

Cad tá ar cois agat? What are you up to?

13. PRÁTAÍ ISTOÍCHE IS PRÁTAÍ SA LÓ IS DÁ n-ÉIREOINN I MEÁNOÍCHE, IS PRÁTAÍ A GHEOBHAINN

Potatoes at night and potatoes by day
And if I rose at midnight, twould be potatoes again.

A little rhyme to remind us of the time when potatoes were the staple of the Irish diet.

BAIN TRIAIL AS

Tháinig sé abhaile um mheán oíche.
He came home at midnight.

14. IS FEARR BEAGÁN DEN GHAOL NÁ MÓRÁN DEN CHARTHANAS

A little kinship is better than a lot of charity. Family connections are important. Blood is thicker than water.

◦◦◦ BAIN TRIAIL AS ◦◦◦

Ní raibh mórán daoine ann.
There weren't many people there.

15. IS Í AN DIAS IS TROIME IS ÍSLE A CHROMAS A CEANN

It's the heaviest ear of corn (*dias*) that bends it head the lowest. Might or strength should always be accompanied by humility.

◦◦◦ BAIN TRIAIL AS ◦◦◦

Tá mé trom tuirseach. I am sad and weary.

16. AN TÉ A THABHARFAS SCÉAL CHUGAT, TABHARFAIDH SÉ DHÁ SCÉAL UAIT

He who brings you a story will take two stories from you. A reference to the time when storytelling was a popular pastime and a storytelling session would involve the swopping of stories (*scéalta*). Stories attract stories.

⤳ BAIN TRIAIL AS ⤵

Dea-scéal nó droch-scéal? Pé scéal é, inis dúinn!
Good news or bad news? Whatever it is, tell us!

17. ÉIST MÓRÁN, CAN BEAGÁN

Listen a lot, say (or sing) little. Solid, practical advice for daily living. Listening is the more difficult skill. Similar to: *Beagán, agus a rá go maith* (A little, and say it well).

Éist liom. Tá mé ag caint leat.
Listen to me. I'm talking to you.

18. AN TÉ NACH nGLACANN COMHAIRLE GLACFAIDH SÉ COMHRAC

He who refuses advice, let him expect trouble. Literally, he who does not take advice will take combat (*comhrac*). Another *seanfhocal* says, *Is ionann comhairle is cúnamh* (Advice is similar to help). And help is preferable to combat any day.

Gabhaim pardún agat. I beg your pardon.

19. TÁ TÚ AG FEADAÍL DUIT FÉIN

You are not in earnest. Literally, you're only whistling to yourself. Not to be trusted.

Téigh ag feadaíl! Go whistle! I don't believe you!

20. DÁ DHOIMHNE AN TOBAR IS EA IS GLAINE AN t-UISCE

The deeper the well, the cleaner the water. If you're seeking the truth, be prepared to dig deep rather than accept what's on the surface.

◦──❧ BAIN TRIAIL AS ❧──◦

Táim domhain ar an gceol sin.
I'm really 'into' that music.

21. SCINNEANN ÉAN AS GACH EALTA

There's a black sheep in every family. Literally, one bird flees every flock. There's always one.

◦──❧ BAIN TRIAIL AS ❧──◦

Scinneann an focal uaim. The word escapes me.

22. IS IOMAÍ LÁ I MBLIAIN IS FICHE IS NÍL LÁ ACU NACH dTAGANN

There are many days in twenty-one years. And every one of them will come. Some will be bright and some will be dark, but all must be experienced. Be patient!

BAIN TRIAIL AS

Tá tú bliain is fiche. Comhghairdeas!
You're twenty-one. Congratulations!

23. IS GIORRA DUIT TIGH DO CHOMHARSA NÁ TIGH DO GHAOLTA

Your neighbour's house is nearer than that of your relations. When troubles come your neighbours may be of more help than your relations, if only because they are nearer to you.

◈ BAIN TRIAIL AS ◈

Tá gaol agam leis. I am related.

24. MAR A BHEID LEAT, BÍ LEO

As they are to you, be likewise to them. Do unto others as you would have them do to you.

◈ BAIN TRIAIL AS ◈

Bí liom ar feadh tamaill.
Be (stay) with me for a while.

25. MÁS MAITH IS MITHID

Not before time! Said to welcome something that is long overdue.

◈ BAIN TRIAIL AS ◈

Is mithid dom imeacht. It's time for me to go.

26. IS MINIC A BHÍ DROCH-CHRÚ FAOI CHAPALL GABHA

The blacksmith's horse is often the worst shod. The craftsman often neglects his own property. Similar to: 'The cobbler's children are often last to be shod.'

⚬ BAIN TRIAIL AS ⚬

Is minic a théim ann. I often go there.

27. TÁ A FHIOS AG AN DOMHAN AGUS TADHG AN MHARGAIDH

Everybody knows. Literally, the world (*domhan*) and the man on the street (*Tadhg an mhargaidh*; Tim of the market) knows. This is no secret.

⚬ BAIN TRIAIL AS ⚬

Ar fud an domhain. All over the world.

28. NÍ CHUIMHNÍTEAR AR AN ARÁN A ITEAR

Eaten bread is soon forgotten. Today's newspaper will be the wrapping for tomorrow's chips. Time moves on and the wonder of the day becomes a one-day wonder.

BAIN TRIAIL AS

Cuimhnítear air gach lá.
He is remembered every day.

29. GURA MAITH AN MHAISE DUIT É

May it turn out for your good. *Maise* means benefit; as in, *Nollaig faoi shéan is faoi mhaise dhuit* (A happy and prosperous Christmas to you).

BAIN TRIAIL AS

Go raibh maith agat. Thank you.

30. TÁ AN LÁMH IN UACHTAR AIGE

He has the upper hand. He is in command. Hence, *uachtarán* means a leader or president.

~ BAIN TRIAIL AS ~

Is maith liom uachtar reoite. I like ice cream.

Focailín

You will surprise yourself at how much you can build your Irish vocabulary around a *Focailín* (little word) like:

Go

Go maith	Well done
Go breá	Lovely
Go ciúin	Quietly
Go tapa	Quickly
Go mall	Slowly
Go láidir	Strongly
Go lag	Weakly
Go dian	Intensely
Go gasta	Quickly
Go hiomlán	Totally

DECEMBER
nollaig

1. NÍ BREAC GO BRUACH É

It's not over until the final whistle. Literally, (in fisherman's terms) it's not a trout until it's landed on the bank. It was this *seanfhocal* used by gaelic games commentator Brian Tyers that prompted me to begin this collection. *Go raibh maith agat, a Bhriain!*

⟿ BAIN TRIAIL AS ⟿

Tá sé lán go bruach. It's full to the brim.

2. AR EAGLA NA hEAGLA

To be sure to be sure! Literally, for fear of fear. To make assurance doubly sure.

Ná bíodh eagla ort. Don't be afraid.

3.   IS BINN BÉAL INA THOST

Silence is golden. Literally, the silent mouth is sweet. At the very least, think before you open your mouth.

Bí i do thost! Be quiet! Hold your tongue!

4.   AN RUD NACH bhFEICEANN SÚIL NÍ BHRÓNANN CROÍ

What you don't know won't hurt you. Literally, what the eye doesn't see won't trouble the heart.

Tá súil agam go mbeidh sé ann.
I expect he will be there.

5. NÍ MAR A SHÍLTEAR BÍTEAR

Things are not what one expects. Appearances can be deceptive and what was expected often doesn't turn out to be the case.

BAIN TRIAIL AS

Síleann siad go bhfuil deireadh leis!
They think it's all over!

6. AN RUD NACH FIÚ É A LORG NÍ FIÚ É A FHÁIL

What's not worth searching for is not worth finding. Don't waste your time in futile pursuits.

BAIN TRIAIL AS

Bhí mé á lorg le tamall.
I was looking for him for a while.

7.   CUIR AN DONAS AR CAIRDE

Put off the evil day. Literally, postpone the misfortune that may be ahead. We have enough on our plate already.

BAIN TRIAIL AS

Cheannaigh mé an rothar ar cairde.
I bought the bike on credit.

8.   NÍ BHÍONN GEARÁN GAN ÁBHAR

There's no smoke with a fire. Literally, there's never a complaint without a reason.

BAIN TRIAIL AS

Ná bí ag déanamh gearáin. Stop complaining.

9. IS MINIC A BHEIR DALL AR GHIORRIA

It's often a blind man (*dall*) catches a hare! An expression of disbelief at some outlandish claim, like 'Pull the other one!' or 'And pigs might fly!'

⟿ BAIN TRIAIL AS ⟿

Táim dall ar an rud sin. I know nothing about that.

10. TÁ SÉ AG FAIRE NA TAOIDE AR AN TRÁ

He is attempting the impossible. Literally, he is trying to keep the tide (*taoide*) away from the strand (*trá*) – just like King Canute of old. It can't be done.

⟿ BAIN TRIAIL AS ⟿

Bí ar d'fhaire! Be on guard!

11. NÍ BHEATHAÍONN NA BRIATHRA NA BRÁITHRE

The brothers/friars (*bráithre*) won't live on fine words (*briathra*). The body must be nourished just as much as the soul. A nice piece of wordplay.

⟡ BAIN TRIAIL AS ⟡

Briathar Dé. The word of God.

12. IS FEARR ÉAN AR LÁIMH NÁ DHÁ ÉAN AR AN gCRAOBH

A bird in the hand is worth two in the bush. Appreciate what you have above what you hope for.

⟡ BAIN TRIAIL AS ⟡

Craobh Peile/Iomána na hÉireann.
The All-Ireland Football/Hurling Championship.

13. IS FEARR GO MALL NÁ GO BRÁCH

Better late than never.

⤛ BAIN TRIAIL AS ⤜

Luath nó mall. Sooner or later.

14. IS UMHAL STIALL DE
LEATHAR DUINE EILE

It's easy to be generous at someone else's expense.
Literally, to give a strip (*stiall*) of someone else's
leather (*leathar*). It's easy to pay the bill when it's
not coming out of your own pocket.

⤛ BAIN TRIAIL AS ⤜

Ní deacair capall umhal a sporadh.
It's not hard to spur a willing horse.

15. NÍ FHAIGHEANN MINIC ONÓIR

What happens often doesn't win any honours. The commonplace is often ignored.

BAIN TRIAL AS

Is mór an onóir dom an corn seo a ghlacadh.
It's a great honour for me to accept this trophy.

16. FUARANN AN GRÁ NACH mBÍONN LÁITHREACH

The love that is not present cools quickly. It's important to keep the flame alight! Not quite the same as 'Absence makes the heart grow fonder'.

BAIN TRIAL AS

Beidh mé ann láithreach. I'll be there straight away.

17. CONAS A BHEADH AN t-ÚILLÍN ACH MAR A BHEADH AN ABHAILLÍN?

The apple doesn't fall far from the tree. Literally, how would the apple be different from the apple tree? It's difficult to escape from our genes.

↪ BAIN TRIAIL AS ↩

Conas atá tú inniu? How are you today?

18. NÍ BHÍONN TRÉAN BUAN

Whatever is strong (or intense) does not last – whether it be weather or a despot. As Shakespeare put it:

Golden lads and girls must
as chimney-sweepers come to dust.

↪ BAIN TRIAIL AS ↩

Tá tréan airgid aige. He has plenty of money.

19. BEIDH OÍCHE GO MAIDIN ACU

They will party all night! Literally, they will have night until morning.

Beidh mé ann ar maidin.
I'll be there in the morning.

20. IS AG DIA IS FEARR A FHIOS

God knows best. Leave it in the hands of the Lord.

Tá a fhios agam/Níl a fhios agam faoi sin.
I know/don't know about that.

21. IS MINIC A BHÍONN CIÚIN CIONTACH

It's often the quiet one that is guilty (*ciontach*). Be wary of the silent one.

⇐ BAIN TRIAIL AS ⇒

Fuarthas ciontach/neamhchiontach é.
He was found guilty/not guilty.

22. NÍ FÉASTA GAN RÓSTA

No feast is complete without a roast. Think of the Christmas dinner without the turkey/goose/chicken.

⇐ BAIN TRIAIL AS ⇒

A leithéid de féasta a bhí again! Such a feast we had!

23. AN TÉ IS MÓ A OSCLÁIONN A BHÉAL IS É IS LÚ A OSCLÁIONN A SPARÁN

He who opens his mouth most opens his purse least. Generous with words, miserly with money. Talk is cheap!

⟋⟋ BAIN TRIAIL AS ⟍⟍

Is é Corcaigh an contae is mó in Éirinn agus is é an Lú an contae is lú. Cork is the biggest county in Ireland and Louth is the smallest.

24. BIA IS DEOCH I gCOMHAIR NA NOLLAG, ÉADACH NUA I gCOMHAIR NA CÁSCA

Food and drink for Christmas and new clothes for Easter. Christmas for feasting, but Easter for dressing up.

Cheannaigh mé prátaí i gcomhair an dinnéir.
I bought potatoes for the dinner.

25. NOLLAIG FAOI SHÉAN IS FAOI MHAISE DUIT

A happy and successful Christmas to you. A common Christmas greeting. And the reply?

~~~ BAIN TRIAIL AS ~~~

Gurab amhlaidh duit féin. And the same to you.

26. IS MÓR É BUÍOCHAS BEAGÁIN AGAT

You give much thanks for the little you receive. A reminder that Christmas is a time for gratitude.

~~~ BAIN TRIAIL AS ~~~

Buíochas le Dia. Thanks be to God.

27. CASTAR NA DAOINE AR A CHÉILE ACH NÍ CHASTAR NA SLÉIBHTE

People meet each other but the mountains never do. For all their solidity and permanence, the mountains never came together, unlike people who meet and interact. Cherish and nourish the human connection.

⟿ BAIN TRIAIL AS ⟾

M'fhear céile/mo bhean chéile. My husband/wife.

28. IS É LÁR DO LEASA É AN TRÁTH IS MEASA LEAT

The worst of times can be the best for you. We can learn from misfortune and resolve to do better.

⟿ BAIN TRIAIL AS ⟾

An rud is measa ar domhan.
The worst thing in the world.

29. NUAIR d'IMIGH AN LEANN,
d'IMIGH AN GREANN

When the drink was gone, the fun was over. A moral for this time of year. Don't depend on drink to provide all the enjoyment.

⟳ BAIN TRIAIL AS ⟲

Is greannmhar an duine é. He's a funny person.

30. IS OLC AN MÁISTIR AN TINE ACH
IS MAITH AN SEIRBHÍSEACH Í

Fire is a good servant but a bad master. It serves us well to provide heat and comfort, but when it goes out of control it can be a deadly master.

⟳ BAIN TRIAIL AS ⟲

Dá olcas é, bhí a mhac níos measa!
As bad as he was, his son was worse!

31. OÍCHE AN DÓTHAIN MHÓIR

The night of full and plenty. New Year's Eve was known as such because it was believed that if you ate enough on this night you would have enough to eat for the coming year. *Athbhliain faoi mhaise duit* (Happy New Year to you). *Agus go mbeirimid beo ar an am seo arís* (May we be hale and hearty this time next year).

⤚ BAIN TRIAIL AS ⤙

Tá mo dhóthain ite/ólta agam!
I have eaten/drunk enough!

Focailín

You will surprise yourself at how much you can build your Irish vocabulary around a *Focailín* (little word) like:

I/In	In
I lár na páirce	In the middle of the field
Tá an suíochán sin in áirithe	That seat is reserved
Bíonn sé ann i gcónaí	He's always there
Tá sé sin i gcoinne an dlí	That's against the law
I ndiaidh an dinnéir	After dinner
I ndeireadh na dála	At the end of it all
Chuaigh mé in éineacht le Róisín	I went in the company of Róisín
Tá mé i ngrá le Róisín	I'm in love with Róisín
I rith an lae	During the day
I bpreab na súl	In the blink of an eye

STOLEN WORDS

Languages readily borrow from each other. Here are twenty-five Irish words that have been anglicised and are common in the English language.

Amadán	A foolish person
A mhic	My son/young man
Bladar	Blather, flattery or coaxing
Blas	A taste, as in a 'a Kerry blas'

Bóithrín	A boreen/little road
Bróg	Brogue, a boot or shoe
Cábóg	A rustic fellow
Cailín	Colleen, a girl
Go leor	Galore, plenty
Geansaí	A gansey or jersey
Geab	Chat, as in 'the gift of the geab'
Gob	A 'gob' or mouth
Gársún	Gossoon, a boy
Loch	A lough or lake
Lúdramán	A lazy, idle fellow
Pincín	A minnow or 'pinkeen'
Poitín	Poteen, an illicit drink
Prátaí	Potatoes or 'praties'
Púca	A 'pooka' or ghost
Ráiméis	Nonsense

Seoinín	Shoneen, an 'aper of foreign ways'
Síbín	A shebeen, An illicit public house
Slíbhín	Slieveen, a sly trickster
Slog	A 'slug' or quick swallow
Smidiríní	Smithereens, little pieces

Do you know any more?

GREETINGS
BLESSINGS
WISHES

———⸺∞⸺———

Twenty-five common examples from the Irish language

Dia duit	God be with you /Hello
Dia is Muire duit (Response)	God and Mary be with you
Togha fir/mná	Sound man/woman!
Maith an cailín	Good girl

Slán leat	Goodbye
Mise le meas	Yours sincerely
Ochón	Alas
Mo bhrón	My sorrow
Oíche mhaith	Goodnight
Codladh sámh	Sleep well
Bail ó Dhia ort/ar an obair	God's blessing on you/on the work
An bhail chéanna ortsa (Response)	And the same to you
Dia linn	God be with us (when someone sneezes)
Fáilte isteach	Welcome in (to the house)
Sláinte	Cheers!
Gaillimh Abú!	Up Galway!
Go bhfóire Dia orainn	God help us
Slán abhaile	Safe home

Go n-éirí an t-ádh leat	May you succeed
Faid ar do shaol	Long life to you
I bhfad uainn an t-olc	May harm be far from us
Go méadaí Dia do stór	May God increase your 'store'
Go maire tú an céad	May you live to be a hundred
Go dtuga Dia ciall duit	May God give you sense
Solas na bhFlaitheas dá anam/dá h-anam	The light of heaven to his/her soul

THE
DICTIONARY
MAN

Fr Patrick Dinneen
(1860–1934)

———◦◦◦———

One of the primary sources for this collection was Fr Patrick Dinneen's Irish–English dictionary, *Foclóir Gaedhilge agus Béarla*, a 'thesaurus of the words, phrases and idioms of the modern language', first published in 1904. It is an extraordinary book and he was an extraordinary man. It is only fitting, therefore, to append this account of his life and work.

Patrick Dinneen was born on Christmas Day 1860, the fifth of ten children, in Rathmore, Co. Kerry. That particular area was known as *Sliabh*

Luachra and contributed much poetry and music to the Irish tradition. Patrick was used to hearing poets recite in his childhood home and his father, a sheep dealer, often took his son with him on his travels, when he would share local lore with the boy. He was a bright boy at school and was taught Latin by the local parish priest. After secondary school at St Brendan's College, Killarney, he moved to Clongowes College, Co. Kildare, following the invitation of a visiting Jesuit priest.

In 1880 he joined the Jesuit order and studied for a degree in English, classics and maths at the Royal University. After ordination he taught in Clongowes and developed a growing interest in the Irish language. A major influence was a Jesuit colleague, Fr McErlean, who introduced him to the riches of Maynooth library. In 1900 Patrick Dinneen resigned from the Jesuit order to devote himself to the study of the Irish language. It was a courageous decision. Although he remained a priest, he was barred from saying Mass because of his 'disobedience'.

His output became prolific. Under the auspices of the Irish Texts Society, he compiled *The Poems of Aodhagán Ó Rathaille* and *The Poems of Eoghan Rua Ó Súilleabháin*, wrote a historical novel and a play and translated Charles Dickens' *A Christmas Carol* and Virgil's *Aeneid*. He began work on a 'pocket' Irish–English dictionary (783 pages), seeking contributions from all over Ireland – not just words and meanings, but also usage and idiom. There was a huge response and the dictionary was published in 1904. The book attracted a lot of criticism, but Dinneen delighted in defending his work vigorously. Unfortunately the plates for this work were destroyed in a printing-house fire in 1916. Dinneen began a ten-year project on a new and revised edition of the dictionary. This edition of 1,300 pages was published in 1927, with the Irish Texts Society acknowledging a government contribution of £1,000 towards the cost of the work, enabling them to sell the book to the public at twelve shillings and sixpence.

While he acknowledged the 'advice, extensive learning, the unflagging energy and zeal' of Mr L.S. Gogan of the National Museum, Dinneen suffered greatly from a lack of resources and compiling a work of this ambition was an amazing feat a century ago. Inevitably, fake word lists were sent to him. He insisted on a multiplicity of meanings for the same word; for example, *maide*, a stick or piece of timber, can also mean an oar, a treadle, a knife-handle, a rooftie, a crutch, a seesaw, a sugarstick, parts of a bed, a hobbyhorse, a stirabout stick, etc., etc.

Alf Mac Lochlainn, former director of the National Library of Ireland described the dictionary as a 'strange book, in some ways an infuriating book, in others an endearing one'.

Dinneen aimed high. In the preface to the 1927 edition, he states, 'The folklore, the habits and beliefs, the songs and tales, the arts and crafts of the people as well as the history, topography and antiquities of the country have been pressed into service to throw light on the meanings of words or to supply words or expressions not previously recorded.'

He was working on a new edition of *The Confession of St Patrick* in 1934 when he took ill and died. He was given a state funeral and is buried in the Poet's Corner in Glasnevin Cemetery, Dublin. A state funeral for a man who was remembered in the National Library as the 'gentle shabby old man chewing apples and raw carrots, with a pile of books around him like a rampart' (Brian Cleeve and Anne Brady, *A Dictionary of Irish Writers*, Dublin: Lilliput, 1985) and who is remembered in his native Rathmore as the Dictionary Man.